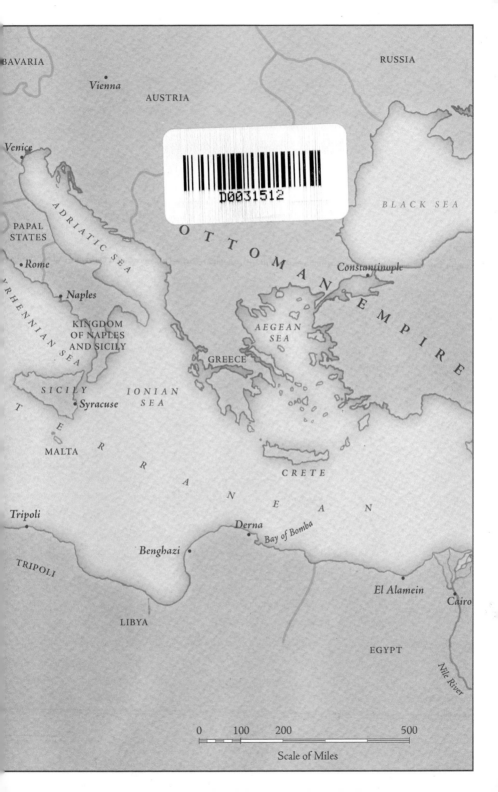

THE BARBARY PIRATES

Burning of the frigate Philadelphia *on the night of the 16th of February, 1804*

From the Halls of Montezuma

To the Shores of Tripoli;

We fight our Country's battles

In the air, on land and sea . . .

U.S. Marine Corps Hymn

THE BARBARY PIRATES

C. S. FORESTER

STERLING PUBLISHING CO., INC.
New York

A FLYING POINT PRESS BOOK

Design: PlutoMedia
Front cover painting: detail from *Decatur Boarding the Tripolitan Gunboat*
by Dennis Malone Carter, Naval Historical Center
Frontispiece and interior map: Naval Historical Center

Library of Congress Cataloging-in-Publication Data

Forester, C. S. (Cecil Scott), 1899-1966.
The Barbary pirates / C.S. Forester. — Updated ed.
p. cm. — (Sterling Point books)
"A Flying Point Press book"—T.p. verso.
Originally published: New York : Random House, 1953.
Includes index.
ISBN-13: 978-1-4027-4142 5 (paper)
ISBN-10: 1-4027-4142-1 (paper)
ISBN-13: 978-1-4027-4522-5 (trade)
ISBN-10: 1-4027-4522-2 (trade)

1. United States—History—Tripolitan War, 1801-1805. 2. Pirates—Africa, North—History—19th century. 3. Pirates—Mediterranean Region—History—19th century. 4. Africa, North—History, Naval—19th century. 5. Mediterranean Region—History, Naval—19th century. I. Title.

E335.F67 2007
973.4'7—dc22

2006031574

2   4   6   8   10   9   7   5   3   1

Published by Sterling Publishing Co., Inc.
387 Park Avenue South, New York, NY 10016
Originally published by Random House, Inc. under the title *The Barbary Pirates*
Copyright © 1953 by C. S. Forester
New material in this updated edition
Copyright © 2007 by Flying Point Press
Map copyright © by Richard Thompson, Creative Freelancers, Inc.
Distributed in Canada by Sterling Publishing
c/o Canadian Manda Group, 165 Dufferin Street
Toronto, Ontario, Canada M6K 3H6
Distributed in the United Kingdom by GMC Distribution Services
Castle Place, 166 High Street, Lewes, East Sussex, England BN7 1XU
Distributed in Australia by Capricorn Link (Australia) Pty. Ltd.
P.O.Box 704, Windsor, NSW 2756, Australia

Printed in China
All rights reserved

Sterling ISBN-13: 978-1-4027-4522-5
ISBN-10: 1-4027-4522-2

For information about custom editions, special sales, premium and corporate purchases, please contact Sterling Special Sales Department at 800–605–5489 or specialsales@sterlingpub.com.

CONTENTS

THE BARBARY PIRATES

CHAPTER 1

PIRATES OFF THE COAST OF NORTH AFRICA!

FOR CENTURIES THE BARBARY PIRATES HAD plagued the world. Long before any settler had set foot in the New World they had begun their raids on merchant vessels.

Cervantes, who later was to write the story of Don Quixote, was a prisoner of the Barbary pirates a generation before Raleigh's colonists landed at Roanoke in 1587. More than a century later Defoe, writing about a popular hero of fiction, Robinson Crusoe, told about his capture by, and escape from, the rovers of Sallee in Morocco.

How did this nuisance begin? Why did the civilized world put up with it for so long?

It should be understood that the Barbary pirates were not pirates in the real sense of the word. They were the citizens of countries which were at war with other countries. They captured prizes and took prisoners just as any warring nation did. At first the Barbary pirates had a religious reason for their wars: they were Muslims and they considered it their duty to make war on the Christians. When the Muslims enslaved their prisoners they were not behaving any worse than their enemies did, for in those days there were no international treaties regarding the treatment of captives.

Later on, when other countries began to observe certain rules in these matters, the Barbary States followed their example to a certain extent. They solemnly declared war and made peace. They kept their prisoners at hard labor and sold them for ransom, but in that hard world of long ago, prisoners could nowhere expect kind treatment. The ransoms that the pirates demanded were like the war indemnities and tribute money demanded in treaties of peace by other countries.

The name *Barbary States* came from a term originally used by the Greeks. Two thousand years before, they had called all those who did not speak Greek "Barbarians." This name was used in an effort to imitate the strange speech of foreigners, and it came to be permanently applied to the people of North Africa, the Berbers.

The homelands of these people—the four North African countries of Morocco, Algiers, Tunis, and Tripoli—were known as the Barbary States. They were parts of the vast Ottoman Empire which at one time had threatened to conquer the whole world. Later, this empire fell to pieces of its own weight, largely because it had never been able to build any system of government except a simple tyranny.

The Ottoman conquest of North Africa had not been very successful. Local generals, governors, and religious leaders managed to set themselves up as independent. At the same time they posed as dutiful subjects of the central government at Constantinople. But their rulers did not have an easy life, even if they lived in the midst of great wealth and enjoyed unlimited power.

The Dey or Bey, Pasha or Emperor, whatever the local ruler called himself, lived only as long as he could remain more powerful than his rivals and enemies. The moment his grasp weakened he could expect to be strangled and to be succeeded by someone else eager to take his place. The truth was that a large part of the people were no more loyal to their rulers than their rulers were to Constantinople. They paid taxes only when the ruler was strong enough to compel them; and they were often hostile and independent under their own chiefs.

It was only in the walled towns, and along the coastal strip, and in the accessible valleys, that the Muslim rulers could enforce their will. The pirate cities were often shut off, with the sea on one side and an enemy countryside on the other. So the rulers living in these seaboard towns came to be dependent for their luxuries, and even for their necessaries, on what they could steal from the outside world. The sea was far more open to them than the mountains and deserts that hemmed them in at their backs. With the loot they could win at sea they could buy their food from neighboring tribes. The slaves they captured could build palaces and fortifications for them, and they were thereby saved from any necessity to do honest work.

So to sea they went, capturing poorly armed ships, and often raiding the Christian coasts to loot the villages. The shores of Italy and France, sometimes even Ireland and once or twice Denmark, saw the Barbary pirates landing to carry off plunder and slaves. They exercised a certain amount of care not to anger powerful nations who might fight back. Often the pirates were glad to accept money instead of plunder, and ransom for the slaves. Up to a point money was more useful to them than either. But only up to a point.

The pirates must have war. Otherwise, the world would soon cease to fear them. Furthermore, among Arab pirates it was considered the mark of a gentleman to go out fighting now and then. So the Deys and the Beys went on raiding peaceful commerce. They knew perfectly well that if they stopped, there would be shortages of necessary goods among their subjects. These people would quickly find a ruler who would promise to manage things better.

Naturally the civilized world did not accept all this looting and piracy without protest. Over and over again European countries sent armed forces to North Africa. Spain and Sicily and France all sent their fleets and sometimes their armies. One of Britain's best admirals, Blake, was sent by Cromwell in the seventeenth century with a fleet that bombarded Tunis and for a short time brought order to the Mediterranean. Repeatedly, the European powers seized portions of North Africa and held them for a time. This was one of the best ways to control the Barbary States, for any Christian foothold in North Africa broke the chain of coastwise navigation that was important to a country of few roads.

Portugal provides another example of the struggle

against the Barbary States. Before Columbus discovered America, Portugal conquered Tangier and held the city for two hundred years. But the further history of the occupation is unfortunately typical. Tangier had to be occupied by Portuguese soldiers to defend it from the attacks of the Moors. Danger was constant and fighting frequent, and the occupation was expensive in money and men, while the returns in terms of trade were poor. The Portuguese could not make the place pay any more than the Moors could without piracy.

In 1662 Portugal was glad to rid herself of the burden by giving Tangier to England as part of the dowry when Charles II married a Portuguese princess. England raised a regiment or two and took over the occupation— the remains of York Castle still stand in Tangier as a reminder of the presence of the duke who later became James II. But twenty years of continuous warfare and siege wore out English patience, and the Dutch wars sapped her strength. In 1684 the garrison was withdrawn and the place reverted to the Moors.

The constant wars in Europe played an important part in allowing the Barbary pirates to continue so long as an expensive nuisance. Countries fighting for their existences could never afford to waste any of their strength on expeditions to Africa. The periods of time between wars were too short to permit long-term action against the pirates, although numerous attempts were made.

These attempts nearly all ended in a bargain being struck, after long haggling. The more powerful the country that was bargaining, the better the terms that were obtained. If the pirates pushed their demands too high the other power would fight sooner than pay. In time the pirates became really skillful in adapting their demands to the situation. They knew just the right sum to ask so that peace would be a little more profitable than war for both sides.

There were certain countries with whom the Barbary States never made peace. At that time, Italy was broken up into numerous tiny states—the Pope ruled Central Italy; Tuscany, Sardinia, Sicily, and Venice were independent, but their governments were mostly feeble and corrupt. As their fleets and their armies were weak, the Barbary States had no fear of them, and preyed on their shipping for centuries.

The pirates also raided their Italian coasts, to give the pirate fleets and their crews practice in looting. This proved to be an important bargaining factor when it came to haggling with the other powers. Moreover, such activities gave the pirates with a taste for fighting a chance to take part in their favorite pastimes without much danger. The raids also gave the pirates a supply of slave labor more convenient than that from across the Sahara desert.

One other factor must be taken into consideration. This state of affairs had lasted for centuries. British merchant ships had been exposed to capture by the pirates ever since the first ones had ventured into the Mediterranean. When the kingdom of France extended its rule to the Mediterranean, the pirates were already there. When Spain and Portugal freed themselves from the Moorish yoke, the new Christian kingdoms found themselves at war with Barbary.

The European shipping owner was inclined to think of losses he suffered at the hands of pirates as something that must be endured, for he had never known anything else. The attacks by the pirates added to working expenses, but so did storms and contrary winds. It seemed useless to hope that any of these evils would come to an end.

Finally, the problem was not an easy one to solve. It was possible for the European powers to bring a temporary halt to the pirates' activities. But for the Barbary States to give up piracy would mean that they would have to change their whole way of life. This was something they could not even consider. Under threats they would promise to keep the peace—they would promise anything. But in time, their lack of money and necessary goods would force them to return to their old way of life.

At the end of the Napoleonic wars, Europe used bombardment and blockade to teach the pirates a lasting lesson. Their slaves were freed, their ships captured, and their fortifications knocked into rubble. The pirates were forced to give promises of good behavior, but they were soon driven by their necessities into piracy again. Finally, France occupied Algiers and then—as had never been possible before—conquered the country foot by foot and replaced barbarism with civilization.

CHAPTER 2

AMERICAN SHIPS CAPTURED

WHEN THE YOUNG AMERICAN REPUBLIC CAME into existence, the situation in the Mediterranean seemed as far from solution as ever. Yet American merchant captains wanted to do business there. Shipping was an industry of vast importance to the young country on the Atlantic seaboard, just as it had been in Colonial days. Both as carriers and as traders American ships could make big profits, thanks to the excellent American shipbuilding facilities and the sharp American business sense.

The Stars and Stripes had not come of age before they were to be seen on every one of the seven seas, and they had no sooner appeared than they ran into trouble. Only a year after America and England signed the peace of 1783, a Moroccan warship, cruising in the Atlantic, captured the American merchant brig *Betsey*. The Moroccan captain had never seen the strange flag before, and it was taken for granted that the Ottoman powers were at war with any Christian nation with whom a treaty of peace had not been signed.

In spite of this occurrence, Morocco was the least troublesome of all the Barbary States. Its Emperor was a member of a long established dynasty and so he was fairly certain of his position. He protected his throne with the aid of a powerful bodyguard of African slave-soldiers who were devoted to him, and he enforced his rule by cruel methods. So the Emperor did not have to defer to the wishes of his ship captains, nor did he go in fear of being strangled if he did not give them the opportunity of taking prizes at sea.

Besides, Morocco, unlike the other Barbary States, controlled a large part of the interior as well as the coast towns, thanks to her comparatively stable government and regular army. So there was a regular food supply. Morrocan farms produced so much that there was a small amount left over for export. There was also a good deal of trade by the caravan routes across the Sahara.

Morocco, in fact, was a trading nation, and the Emperor saw the possibility of extending trade by friendship with America. He was willing to make a treaty; and one was finally signed. Captain Erving and his crew and the *Betsey* had lain captive at Tangier no more than six months before they were released. In the old sailing ship days, that was not much worse than anything else a seaman might expect in the ordinary practice of his profession.

The whole cost of the treaty between Morocco and the United States was no more than ten thousand dollars. This was a relatively small amount, for diplomatic relations with even a Christian power always involved much giving of jeweled snuff boxes and much paying of fees to minor officials. At any rate, the Emperor of Morocco was able to boast that he was the first neutral to recognize the existence of the United States.

Our relations with the pirate state of Algiers were quite different. The Algerine corsairs were hungry for loot. During the recent war, ships had sailed in convoy and pickings had been meager. Immediately after the conclusion of peace, Spain had turned all the weight of her navy upon the Algerines. She had barred Algerine ships from going out into the Atlantic through the Straits of Gibraltar, and had generally acted with so much resolution that they had been glad to make peace.

But peace once more opened the Straits to the Algerines and in the summer of 1785 the *Maria* of Boston and the *Dauphin* of Philadelphia were captured and brought into Algiers. They were the ships of a new and not very important country, which would provide welcome plunder and could not be expected to hit back. Algiers rejoiced when the prizes were brought in—there was always a celebration on those occasions. Then the ships and cargoes were sold and the crews set to forced labor.

Christian slaves were always greatly desired because the Muslims did not like to hold other Muslims in slavery. The captives were forced to do the degrading work which was considered beneath the dignity of an Algerine pirate. Furthermore, to treat the Christians harshly and to feed and house them badly was satisfying to Muslim feelings, and had the advantage of prompting the prisoners to write letters home with moving descriptions of their sufferings. As a result of these letters, the captives' relations or friends or government would gladly pay heavy ransoms for them.

The prisoners wrote to the American consul at Cadiz (their nearest fellow citizen), to friends at Lisbon, and ended by petitioning Congress. Nevertheless, they stayed in prison, such of them as did not die of disease, for eleven years. For at this moment the young republic was groping about to find a form of government; it had neither money nor power.

America did what little she could under the handicaps that beset her. She appealed to her former allies, France and Spain, and by their protests they actually succeeded in having the prisoners in Algiers treated a little better. But it was hopeless to expect either country to do more, to find money or fleets for a country that would make no attempt to provide them for itself.

Jefferson proposed the formation of a league of the smaller powers to establish a fleet which would keep the Barbary Coast under constant blockade. Half a dozen governments were agreeable. But the suggestion came to an end when the United States had to admit that she had no money, no ships, and no men to contribute. The other countries came to the natural conclusion that America was trying to get them to do her work for her, and the league fell apart.

Portugal, as it happened, was playing an important part at this moment. She had chosen to go to war with Algiers rather than continue to pay tribute, and surprisingly enough, Portugal was able to make herself respected in the naval war that followed. She took over the blockade of the Straits of Gibraltar and made it impossible for the Algerine corsairs to enter the Atlantic. At last American shipping could sail that ocean in safety.

As for the Mediterranean itself, the ingenuity and skill

of the American merchant captains prevented further trouble for a time. The Dutch and the Portuguese and the Spaniards were protecting the ships of their own nations with their own ships of war. There was nothing to prevent an American ship from sailing with such convoys and getting protection for nothing. Moreover British ships carried passes, and those passes were an absolute protection, thanks to British naval strength and well-judged bribes. An American skipper who was worth his salt could forge a pass, or bring an old one up to date.

Thus, trade was able to continue without any more Americans being brought into the Algerian slave pens, and the question never became serious enough to compel action by the United States. This was unfortunate for the prisoners already in Algerine hands.

It would have been very little comfort for those prisoners to know what their government was doing for them. Now and then the American government was making an offer. Algiers demanded sixty thousand dollars ransom; America offered four thousand, and would have found it hard to raise even that sum. Jefferson and Adams reported that peace with all the four Barbary States might be purchased for a million dollars, but Congress would appropriate only eighty thousand, so the prisoners stayed in prison.

A final step was to approach one of the several religious orders in France that devoted themselves to the ransoming of Christians from the Barbary States and to request them to undertake the task that the government felt incapable of doing itself. The negotiations dragged on slowly, for bids and counter-bids had to be carried across the Atlantic by sailing ship. Another reason for slowness was that all details had to be kept secret. If it became known how much America was willing to pay to free her citizens the Algerines would raise their price to that limit. Then all American citizens captured in the future would have to be ransomed at the same figure.

At last a series of events broke the deadlock. America adopted the Constitution, which made it possible for her to deal with kidnappers and blackmailers as they ought to be dealt with. Then the French Revolution brought about the breakup of the religious orders in France.

Finally all Europe burst into war. British sea power kept the French merchant ships in their ports except for occasional blockade runners. England's merchant fleets and those of her allies were forced to sail in convoys for protection against French privateers which were far more numerous and dangerous than the corsairs of the Barbary pirates.

As always in war, neutral shipping began to make increased profits. Every warring country needed ships to carry troops and warlike stores, but the need to travel in convoys slowed down the merchant fleets' activities. As a result freight rates rose while the neutrals, unhampered by convoy, reaped the advantage. Neutral ships could make still more money if they were willing to risk capture while blockade-running and contraband-carrying. At the same time the countries that were at war felt a greatly increased need for the neutrals' raw materials and manufactured goods. With this golden market open to her, Portugal could not afford to waste any time fighting

Algiers. Instead she made it her business to buy a hasty peace.

Strangely enough, this unimportant event, a peace between Portugal and Algiers, had a part in bringing about the foundation of the United States Navy.

Heretofore, the Portuguese had prevented the Algerines from passing through the Straits of Gibraltar. Now, with peace, the Straits were once more opened and the Algerines swarmed into the Atlantic. They had been long penned in, first by the Spaniards and then by the Portuguese, and they needed booty and slaves. They knew that in the Atlantic they would find both in plenty; there they would find the ships of a country that had not a single man-of-war to avenge an insult or to offer a moment's protection to her citizens.

At the end of 1793 appalling news began to arrive in the United States. A dozen American ships had been captured, ships from Philadelphia and New York and Newburyport. The Algerines had poured on board them, chattering and shouting in their unknown tongue, their

Oriental robes flapping and their Oriental beards flying in the wind. Madly intent on personal plunder, they had fallen upon the unfortunate Americans and stripped them of all they had.

The reason was this: The pirates had to give an account of all captured ships, cargoes, and crews to the Dey, who claimed his percentage. But the personal possessions of the crews were the prize of the first-comers. Watches and sextants and money were of enormous value, but shirts, trousers and shoes were also precious to the penniless pirates from Algiers. The Americans had to yield everything, in utter submission, for a word of protest would be answered by a blow from a scimitar.

There was no chance of offering any resistance. The American ships, even if they carried a gun or two (few of them did), had crews of only ten or twenty men, while the heavily armed Algerines often had crews of as many as two hundred. Their ships of war were fast and agile. In any case they usually managed to get within close range of their victims by hoisting false colors. People aboard vessels which were attacked knew that if they tried to fight, or if any pirate were hurt, every man in the captured ship would have his throat cut.

There was nothing to do but submit and be taken back to Algiers. There the captives were flung into a filthy prison, given starvation rations and set to work at heavy labor, with the lash for the sick and the weak. There was nothing to do but submit, and to write letters home pleading for rescue or ransom.

When the news of the acts of piracy arrived, America was better prepared to act on it. Reports came in from the American minister to Portugal and the American consul at Lisbon, telling of the losses. The Portuguese government had been persuaded to send some of their warships out as convoy for American vessels, but this was a favor that could not be expected to last for long.

The American minister to Portugal, writing to the Secretary of State, expressed a blunt truth. "It appears absurd to trust to the fleets of Portugal to protect our trade." He went on to say, "If we mean to have a commerce we must have a naval force to defend it."

Even Captain Richard O'Brien, the commander of the

Dauphin who had been a prisoner in Algiers since 1785, wrote stoutly to say that only in strength lay safety. John Paul Jones could be quoted, too. He had, of course, been consulted years before, and just before his death he had advised that the United States should act alone and with a naval force.

The arguments gathered force as they were presented to Congress. But the citizens who were opposed to our building an army and navy were still powerful and quite sincere. They were men of learning and experience who believed that the creation of a regular armed force would endanger the freedom of the republic. They believed that an "officer caste" or a successful commander might one day take over the government of the United States. They believed, too, that because this danger existed, it would be better for the United States to go on enduring the enslavement of her citizens and the loss of her ships.

There was another section of the opposition—James Madison was its spokesman—who believed that the establishment of a navy might lead to difficulties with other naval powers. These men did not give enough thought to the difficulties that might arise in the absence of a navy.

The opposition was strong enough to force a change in the proposed law: If peace were to be made with Algiers, then the work on the ships authorized by the law was to stop. With that concession, the bill passed, and in March, 1794, the United States Navy was born. The President was given the power to start building six frigates. Congress was careful to prescribe what officers and men were to be employed, how they were to be fed, and how much they were to be paid.

Later on, Congress took the final step of appropriating two-thirds of a million dollars for the expenses of the navy. Thereupon the *United States,* the *Constellation,* the *Constitution,* and the other ships which were to make naval history came into being.

Time was to prove that Congress, with all its care, had not troubled to legislate on a most important matter. By not troubling, Congress made another great contribution to naval history. The lawmakers had neglected to name the person who was to design the vessels. The credit for the nomination must go to President Washington, and we first hear the great names of Joshua Humphreys and of his assistant, Josiah Fox.

All countries occasionally pass through periods when they produce a whole generation of great figures. During these periods, outstanding men and women appear in every human activity and add luster to the arts of peace as well as to the arts of war. The Elizabethan Age in England produced men of genius of all kinds, and so did the Revolutionary period in America. Franklin and Washington, Jefferson and Hamilton and Madison—there is no end to the list of men of superlative talent and character.

The name of Joshua Humphreys must be added to the list, as the outstanding designer of warships of his period. He had the clarity of vision that enabled him to decide exactly what type of ship would best serve the purpose of his country, and he had the technical skill and knowledge to carry out his ideas. It was almost equally important that he had the persuasive power and the personality

26

that enabled him to induce other people to agree with him.

Humphreys built ships that were made to endure both battle and storm. He packed them full of fighting power, and he gave them the speed and maneuverability which enabled them to overtake the weak and escape from the strong. At a time when every country in the world was fighting for national existence and calling upon its naval designers to build better ships, it was Humphreys who came forward with the best designs. He produced the ships; it was for America to produce the men.

CHAPTER 3

U.S. ATTEMPTS BLOCKADE OF TRIPOLI HARBOR

A VERY UNHAPPY CHAPTER IN AMERICAN history came gradually to a close. The period of uncertainty and doubt came to an end. At various times government leaders had decided to fight rather than pay blackmail to the Barbary States—but they had continued to pay the blackmail. They had decided, too, that it would be wrong to make payments in the form of naval stores, for the Barbary States would use these against American vessels—but they had sent the naval stores: weapons, ammunition, supplies, even ships.

They had even searched Europe for jeweled pistols

and daggers that might suit the taste of the African rulers. They had submitted more than once to having American merchant ships captured and American citizens enslaved. They had endured the crowning humiliation of seeing an American frigate obeying the orders of the Dey of Algiers to carry presents for him to Constantinople.

Now and then the government of the United States had taken action to avenge these injuries. However, the action lacked force because President Jefferson decided that he could not, under the Constitution, consider the United States to be at war with Tripoli, even though Tripoli was at war with the United States. The result of this was seen when the schooner *Enterprise* fell in with the Tripolitan ship of war *Tripoli,* outmaneuvered her, fought her, beat her into a wreck and forced her to surrender, and then allowed her to go free again.

The Constitution was young then, and it was every man's duty to be as careful about it as he could be. It was only six months later—in February, 1802—that Congress solved the problem by authorizing the President to take whatever action he thought necessary for the protection of the seamen and commerce of the United States.

It was then that an extra word appeared in the orders given by the Secretary of the Navy to the naval officers of the United States. They were ordered to "take, sink, burn, or otherwise destroy" the ships of the enemy. That very phrase had appeared for centuries in the orders given to officers of the British Navy. The extra word "take" made all the difference. Until then our naval officers were ordered only to sink, burn, and destroy, which was one more example of the difficulties that must arise in a badly defined international situation.

In 1801 Tripolitan captains could save their ships and themselves simply by surrendering. This strange situation existed, despite the fact that three months before the battle, the Pasha of Tripoli had declared war on the United States and had insulted the American flag. These events took place after the Pasha had had five years of peace. Almost his first act in 1796, when he succeeded his father (and murdered one brother and drove another out of the country), had been to make peace. Now he felt that he had not made nearly so profitable a bargain as had his neighbors of Morocco and Algiers and Tunis. He hoped war would be more profitable.

Already, in anticipation of trouble with the Pasha, the United States government had taken precautionary steps. A squadron of American ships had been ordered to the Mediterranean. Thus, the United States was brought face to face with a whole series of naval problems which demanded solution. The first one—where to get the necessary ships—was already solved, for vessels were available. Although the 1796 treaty of peace between the United States and Tripoli had been signed before the ships which Humphreys designed were completed, some of them were nearly finished. President Washington had then persuaded Congress to authorize completion, and the others were finished as a result of the brief war with France in 1798 and 1799.

Now, no one doubted that the small squadron which could be sent immediately was large enough to command the Mediterranean—that was the clearest proof of the weakness of the Barbary powers. Everyone knew that if the pirates contested the command of the sea in a pitched battle they would be beaten, which makes it stranger still that the world had tolerated this nuisance for so many centuries.

So there were enough ships; the next thing was to find officers to command them, and that was more difficult. The service was young, but several of the captains were already too old to endure the hardships of long service at sea. Furthermore, the Navy suffered a severe blow when Thomas Truxtun, who in the *Constellation* had so brilliantly captured the *Insurgente* in 1799, refused the command on a point of etiquette.

America had to hunt for a new commander of the Navy, and eventually employed five during the four years that the war lasted. That is not a surprising fact, for men fit for independent command are hard to find. The difficulties regarding the command in the Mediterranean came to the government's notice only as the war progressed. It appeared when the war began that Richard Dale, who as a very young man had been first lieutenant of Paul Jones's *Bonbomme Richard*, was quite suitable, and he became the first commander of the Navy. There were also many junior officers whose brilliance was guessed at if not already proved.

The officers could be found; it was a little harder to find the men. Most of them had to be trained seamen, for the sailing ship seaman was a highly skilled craftsman. Habitually when he went aloft to set sail or to shorten sail he performed feats which equaled those of circus performers. Often he had to perform those feats in the dark, high up in the rigging of a ship that rolled and pitched wildly in a rough sea. Often, too, every rope and piece of canvas that he laid hands on was covered with ice.

To steer a ship in good weather on a steady course so as to lose neither time nor distance was an art hard to learn. To do so in a storm with everyone's safety depending on quick and exact handling of the wheel called for years of experience.

The seaman was a man of a hundred skilled trades. Even making the best use of one's weight and strength in a team working a windlass or hauling on a rope was a knack that had to be acquired. A very brief training would make a man a gunner, but a man could not be called a seaman without at least a year at sea.

So to man the warships of the United States the seamen were necessary, and it was not easy to attract seamen into the service. With the wartime boom, merchant seamen were enjoying good wages and full employment. Consequently, they thought twice about giving up these advantages in exchange for the lower pay authorized by Congress and submitting themselves to the severe discipline of a ship of war and enduring the additional hardships of long months at sea.

There were patriotic men who enlisted for the one-year engagement that the Navy offered, but the numbers had to be filled up with whatever men came to hand. In this latter group were men who could not, for various reasons, find employment in merchant ships and foreign seamen whose usual wages and living conditions were even lower than those in the United States Navy. There were also landsmen who would have to be taught. Dale's instructions from the Secretary of the Navy included a hint that he could "accept the services" of any prisoners of war who might volunteer.

When the ships with their officers and men and stores were ready, it had to be decided how Dale was to use them. It would be foolish to sail such a fleet four thousand miles to Tripoli without a clear idea of what it was to do on arrival there. The Pasha had to be forced to agree to American terms; what was the best method of exerting force? Capturing Tripolitan ships would be effective, but the moment the alarm was given, every Tripolitan ship that could not get home would seek shelter in a neutral harbor. What next?

It might seem obvious that the next thing to do would be to enter the Tripolitans' harbor, capture the shipping there, and threaten to lay the whole place in ruins. But that was not so easy; the harbor was guarded by batteries and fortifications with scores of heavy guns. Wooden ships fighting stone walls were at a sad disadvantage.

The harbor, too, was shallow and difficult to enter, and the Tripolitans had a flotilla of gunboats. These were small craft that carried only one or two heavy guns, but those guns could send their shot even through the stout sides of the *President*. The gunboats were of shallow draft, and they could be moved about by oars, so that they could take shelter among shoals where the American frigates could not reach them. So bombardment of the town was likely to be dangerous and expensive and it might well fail. The orders to Dale did not contemplate bombardment.

The real weakness of Tripoli, which dictated the plan of campaign, was the dependence of the town on outside sources of supply. The roads into the town were bad, so foodstuffs were habitually brought in by sea. If no ships were allowed to enter, the town would have no more food than could be collected in the immediate neighborhood. It was hoped that starvation would soon bring the Tripolitans to their senses.

Grain and meat were imported into Tripoli from various points along the coast, from Italy and Spain, while fishing played an important part in the Tripolitan economy. At that time and for centuries before, the tunny fisheries on the Libyan coast were a productive industry as they are to this day. Bottling up the fishing fleets and cutting off the coasting trade should be effective.

And the Tripolitans depended on the sea for their luxuries as well as their necessities; blockade would keep the corsairs idle, and there would be no more gala days to celebrate the arrival of prizes. The pirate captains who had a voice in the government of the city would not like that, and if they grew restless the Pasha could fear dethronement and assassination.

So the orders to Dale directed him to sweep the enemy's ships from the sea and then to establish a blockade of Tripoli. He was to maintain the blockade until the enemy was willing to agree to terms of peace. Nobody believed that the blockade would be difficult to enforce, or that it would have to be long maintained. Thus it would be inexpensive—especially inexpensive in lives—and the United States government confidently expected that a cheap and easy victory would be won. A summer's campaign ought to humble the Tripolitans. No one stopped to wonder why, if it was as easy as that, the

Barbary pirates had managed to exist for centuries in the face of the hostility of the rest of the world.

There were special reasons which were not easy to appreciate at first. The principal one was geographical. The North African coast is difficult and dangerous. Shallows extend far out, and there are very few harbors. When the wind blew from the sea to the shore—as it did more often than not—a sailing ship was in grave danger of being forced aground. The danger was made greater still because there were no reliable charts and because the shore lay so low and was so featureless that it was hard to determine one's position. A north wind meant terrible danger, and a south wind was likely to blow the blockading ships away from their station.

The coasting and fishing vessels that supplied Tripoli with food were very small. They could creep along in the shallows out of reach of the big ships, and in a calm they would use their oars. By the aid of their local knowledge they could make their final run into the town at night, out of sight of the blockaders. Even a small flow of provisions into the town would make a big difference in the situation there. If only half the usual supply came in, and there were six months' provisions on hand, the town could endure a year of blockade. It could hold out far longer if the people made a sharp cut in their use of food and other necessities. And Dale's seamen were only enlisted for a year!

The other geographical difficulty arose from the distance between the Mediterranean and America. A ship did well if she arrived off Tripoli a month after leaving Hampton Roads. After Dale reached the Mediterranean, it took two months, and often longer, for him to receive a reply to any letter he wrote to his government. Every cannon ball he fired, every barrel of beef his men ate, had to be replaced from four thousand miles away. Sails and cordage wore out fast when continually at sea. If the *Constitution* were to split a topsail in a squall, Dale could count himself lucky if three months later he received a new one.

What Dale needed was an "advance base" somewhere close to Tripoli where stores could be accumulated, his ships refitted, and his men rested. But there was no place in Africa at all suitable, and if there had been it would have taken a military garrison to hold it secure.

There were plenty of friendly ports in the Mediterranean, and the European powers were friendly to Dale's squadron, but Europe was convulsed with war. The ports under British control were hard put to it to supply the British Navy. The ports under French control had been blockaded by the British for years and were experiencing the worst of wartime shortages. When most of the world was locked in desperate combat it could hardly be expected that anyone could spare help for the little American squadron.

For it was only a little squadron—the *President,* the *Philadelphia,* the *Essex,* and the *Enterprise,* a big frigate, two small ones, and a schooner. The squadron was big enough to command the Mediterranean and to scare every Tripolitan ship of war into harbor, but it was not big enough to conduct a war. There were only four ships. Suppose one was employed watching Algiers and Gibraltar, a second was convoying American merchant ships, and a third ran aground and damaged herself—as actually happened to the *Constitution*—how was the blockade to be conducted when the fourth ship ran short of water and had to go off for more? And how were messages to be sent? How was contact to be maintained with the other Mediterranean powers?

Those were problems which Dale had to try to solve, and they were also the problems which faced the American people and the American government. They had entered into a war, and, as happens ninety-nine times out of a hundred, they had underestimated the effort necessary to win it. It remained to be seen if they would have the resolution to see the business through.

CHAPTER 4

COMMODORE MORRIS FAILS TO SUBDUE PIRATES

EVEN THOUGH DALE EVENTUALLY DID BADLY with the forces under his command, he began astonishingly well. He came into Gibraltar in the nick of time after having spent a month crossing the Atlantic. Nelson once said, "Lose not an hour" and Dale's arrival was one more example of the importance of hours in naval warfare, for in Gibraltar he found two Tripolitan ships on the point of going out into the Atlantic to capture prizes.

These ships were under the command of the most formidable of the Tripolitan captains, a European who, taken prisoner by the Tripolitans years before, had changed his religion and his name. He was now called Murad the pirate instead of Peter Lisle the Scot, just as his flagship, which had once been the *Betsey* of Boston, was now the *Meshuda,* twenty-eight guns.

Had Dale been even a day later Murad would have been loose in the Atlantic and could have done very great damage. As it was, Dale came sailing in, saluted the British authorities in Gibraltar, anchored beside Murad, and announced his intention of fighting the pirate the moment he put his nose outside neutral waters. Murad said there was no war as yet (though two months before the Pasha of Tripoli had declared war and cut down the American consular flag), but Dale did not believe him. He left the *Philadelphia* to watch Murad while he himself went on with the rest of the squadron into the Mediterranean.

Murad with his two ships looked out at the *Philadelphia* and did not like what he saw. The British authorities, while they maintained the neutrality of the harbor, would not lift a finger to help him. His stores and water threatened to run short, he faced destruction outside the bay and ruin inside, and in the end abandoned his ships, leaving them in charge of a small maintenance party. He then scuttled across the Straits with his crews in the ships' boats. From Tetuan he and his men tried to get back to Tripoli, but Murad was one of the few who succeeded. For years after, his ships swung useless at their anchors in Gibraltar Bay. Thus, at least a third of the Tripolitan fleet was disposed of.

Dale went on up the Mediterranean, showed his formidable ships of war to Algiers and Tunis, making a very healthy impression, and then proceeded to Tripoli.

So here he was, at the enemy's gates, so to speak. What next? Tripoli was decidedly alarmed. The Tripolitan batteries were manned, the gunboats took shelter under their protection, and the coasting vessels hid themselves away.

Dale with only one ship, the *President,* had been able to make the pirates tremble. The *Philadelphia* he had left at Gibraltar; the *Essex* was on convoy duty. The schooner *Enterprise* began to run short of water and was sent off to Malta to fill up.

Alone, Dale waited for Tripoli to offer peace; Tripoli waited to see what would happen. For two and a half weeks the two sides looked at each other. Now the *President* was running short of water—it was five weeks since she had filled up at Gibraltar—and in Dale's opinion there was nothing else to do but to go to Malta himself to obtain more.

So it was that one morning the astonished Tripolitans looked out over the Mediterranean to find that the coast was clear. The big American frigate had gone. Horsemen took the news along the coast; soon provisions would once more enter Tripoli.

Not only that; the *President* had barely left when a battered ship came creeping into Tripoli under a single sail. She was the *Tripoli,* with thirty wounded on board, having thrown twenty dead overboard, her sides torn with shot and one mast missing. Lieutenant Andrew Sterrett, commanding the *Enterprise,* had encountered her on his way to Malta, and by the brilliant way in which he had handled his ship had utterly defeated her without losing a man himself. The Tripolitans heard the news about the fighting capacity of the Americans with some dismay. On the other hand, there was the astonishing fact that the Americans had set the ship free after capturing her. They had not looted the vessel, and they had not enslaved the crew.

The Tripolitans could hardly be expected to understand the Constitution of the United States or to appreciate Mr. Jefferson's regard for it. They could only reach the conclusion that the Americans knew nothing about waging war, and that they could look forward to wringing more blackmail from this unwarlike nation.

The Tripolitans did not worry at all when American ships showed up now and then to continue the blockade—whenever Dale had a ship available. And before a month was out they had a fresh example of the trusting innocence of these Americans.

Dale, returning from Malta, met a Greek ship heading for Tripoli. He turned her back, in accordance with the laws of blockade. (He could not make her a prize, as she could claim that the news of the blockade had not reached her.) But on board there were forty Tripolitan passengers, including an officer and twenty soldiers. Dale took them prisoners, and then actually landed them all in exchange for the Pasha's promise that he would give three Americans in exchange. There were no American prisoners in Tripoli at the time, and the Pasha's promise was worth no more than any pirate promise in any case.

There could be nothing more encouraging for the Tripolitans. An enemy who proclaimed a blockade and did not enforce it, who took prizes and then returned them, who took prisoners and then set them at liberty, was not an enemy to be feared. Presumably he was therefore an enemy who could be bullied into paying substantial blackmail. Was it not well known that America was sending to the other Barbary States a steady stream of presents—money, jewels and naval stores? The spirits of the Tripolitans rose steadily; so did their demands, and so did their determination to fight it out until those demands were satisfied.

The other Barbary States, who of course had been watching the contest with the deepest interest, began to grow restless. They began to think that they were not being paid enough by the United States. They grew more and more exacting in their demands. They objected to the small hindrance imposed on their trade by Dale's blockade of Tripoli. American consuls were treated with increasing insolence, and ships of war began to be fitted out in the ports of Morocco and Algiers and Tunis.

The unfortunate Dale, as if he had not already enough to worry him, was now alarmed by these menaces. His tiny force had been too small even to watch one single port in the Mediterranean; he could not hope to watch half a dozen more.

Another of his worries resulted from the quick passage of time. Many of his men in the *President* had begun their one year's enlistment as early as April, 1801. Now it was February, 1802, and at that time of year, with the westerly gales blowing, it might take two months or more for his ships to return to America from far inside the Mediterranean. The engagements the United States had entered into with her seamen must be honored.

So Dale sailed for home with his flagship, depriving his

squadron of their leader, and leaving his captains to quarrel with each other. They also quarreled with the United States consuls, who were not only trying to conduct negotiations but were also trying to press plans of campaign of their own devising upon them. It was a miserable end to Dale's command.

But Dale arrived in the United States to find America resolved not only to go on with the blockade, but to exert herself even more in the endeavor to find an honorable peace. More ships were being fitted out; a new commodore had been selected—Richard V. Morris—and no fewer than seven more frigates were destined for service in the Mediterranean. Dale's largest force had amounted to five frigates and a schooner; Morris would have twelve frigates and a schooner if every ship joined him. Surely with that force he could accomplish everything necessary in the Mediterranean, especially now that Congress had empowered the President to fight against America's declared enemies.

America was convinced, as she watched Morris sail away, that this new expedition would soon come home victorious. So profound was this conviction that the administration, suddenly alarmed about the cost of all this, decided that Morris's force was over-large, and recalled two of his frigates.

Morris sailed out from Norfolk in May, 1802, but with contrary winds did not succeed in getting clear of Hampton Roads for two days. He took just four weeks to cross the Atlantic, and arrived at Gibraltar with his ship, the *Chesapeake,* in need of refitting. It was fortunate that at this moment England was at peace with Napoleon, and so all the facilities of the dockyard at Gibraltar were put at Morris's disposal. Three weeks' hard work were required to get the *Chesapeake* ready for sea again and to replace her cracked mainmast, for the United States dockyards had not done their work well.

And while Morris waited at Gibraltar, one item of news reached him after another, each more harassing than the one before. Morocco was threatening trouble. Her Emperor wanted to resume trade with Tripoli, and he wanted to take possession of the *Meshuda*—once the

Betsey of Boston—which was still lying in Gibraltar Bay in charge of Tripolitan caretakers. Morris refused. There was no sense in blockading Tripoli and yet allowing Moroccan ships to enter, nor was there any sense in permitting an increase in the naval strength of a possible enemy.

Morocco was enraged at the refusals. She threatened war, and the American consul, who knew his duty was first to keep peace between Morocco and America, became alarmed and pelted Morris with protests.

That was not the end of Morris's trouble. There were numerous American ships inside or just outside the Mediterranean. It was Morris's business to provide convoy for them, but he simply did not have enough ships to do so and still watch Morocco. The American captains naturally refused to keep out of danger because they would thereby lose profits. So it was not long before news arrived that the *Franklin* of Philadelphia had been taken by a Tripolitan corsair which had slipped out of Tripoli and returned with four American prisoners.

Now Tripoli could apply still greater pressure upon

the United States. Of course no one in Tripoli paid any attention to the Pasha's old agreement with Dale over the twenty Tripolitan prisoners Dale had returned.

Other news came in—trouble and more trouble. Captain Alexander Murray in the *Constellation* had had a skirmish with the Tripolitan gunboats. He had found them close inshore and had exchanged shots with them, but they had made their way back into Tripoli despite his efforts, thanks to favorable weather conditions and the protection afforded them by the shoals. Murray wrote in despair that it was hopeless to try to maintain the blockade without plenty of small craft that were able to go into the shallows after the enemy.

On and on ran his complaints. He was running short of food and water. He did not like the thought of trying to maintain the blockade through the winter. He was quite sure the best thing to do was to give up the blockade and buy peace with Tripoli on whatever terms could be obtained.

So one of Morris's captains was writing to him in this vein. Another never wrote at all—Captain George Little

McNeill of the *Boston,* who went wandering off around the Mediterranean without reporting to him. And the other captains all reported that they needed provisions and water—always that need—and often that their ships were in need of repair.

The orders that reached Morris from the Secretary of the Navy were actually three months old and did not lighten his burden at all. The next orders, two and a half months old, increased his burden by ordering home the *Chesapeake* and the *Constellation.*

Meanwhile, Morris's high-spirited officers were quarreling with one another. Stephen Decatur's brother-in-law, a captain of Marines, was killed in a duel with one of the lieutenants of the *Constellation.* That was only one duel out of many. The next development was a duel between Midshipman Joseph Bainbridge and the secretary of the Governor of Malta. The secretary was killed, thanks to Decatur, who as second, insisted that the men should fight at four yards, so close that the inexperienced midshipman could not miss. This was a troublesome triumph, for Morris depended upon Malta for provisions and water and dockyard facilities, and it was hardly tactful to kill the governor's secretary while in need of the hospitality of Malta. It was one more worry for Morris, who had to send Decatur and Bainbridge back to the United States.

Trouble and more trouble! Swedish ships of war and Danish ships of war came sailing up the Mediterranean. They had been sent, apparently, by their governments to bring the Barbary pirates to order, but Morris could not persuade their admirals to make a clear statement regarding their intentions. Having come, they next disappeared without notice, unable to maintain themselves so far from their bases.

The fragile Peace of Amiens, signed by France, England, Spain and Holland, broke up, and half of Europe was at war again. Convoys and privateers and fighting fleets of all nations once more ranged the Mediterranean, and no one knew from one day to another who was neutral and who was at war. The warring nations now had little to spare to help the Americans, and the neutrals were terrified of offending Napoleon and consequently were careful to do nothing at all.

Morris was overwhelmed with troubles. The *Enterprise* needed caulking and re-coppering; the *Chesapeake,* whose mainmast had been defective, now found that her bowsprit was rotten. In spite of everything, Morris continued to convoy American ships. He battled with gales. He sent home the numerous men whose terms of enlistment had expired, and he tried to replace them with others from Mediterranean ports—not easy in a world at war. He transferred himself to the frigate *New York* and within a month the ship was half wrecked as the result of the accidental explosion of some gunpowder below decks. Luckily it was not the main powder store, or Morris and the *New York* would never have been heard of again. As it was, he had to ask help of the Malta dockyard again.

In all the eighteen months Morris was in the Mediterranean he spent scarcely one-tenth of that time fighting the real enemy, Tripoli. There were excuses in plenty for the delays and the inactivity. In war there are always excuses to be found for doing nothing, but wars are won by the men who can think of reasons for action.

The delay at Malta was brightened by the arrival of Captain John Rodgers's small frigate *John Adams* with a prize. It was that same *Meshuda,* once the *Betsey* of Boston, which had lain so long at Gibraltar, and had been weakly allowed to be taken over by the Emperor of Morocco. This ruler showed his gratitude by filling the *Meshuda* with naval stores for Tripoli, but he chose his moment badly. Rodgers, who arrived on the scene unexpectedly, seized her as a blockade runner; she made no attempt to fight.

Perhaps it was this small success that stimulated Morris into activity. The repairs to the *New York* were completed in three weeks, and Morris sailed again for Tripoli with his two frigates and the *Enterprise.* Fortune favored him, and he arrived to find a dozen coasters laden with grain approaching the port. They were convoyed by the Tripolitan gunboats. Morris moved in to the attack, and then hesitated. The gunboats escaped into Tripoli.

The coasters were hauled on shore while a brigade of the Tripolitan army was hurriedly marched out to guard them.

David Porter, lieutenant on the *New York,* pressed for instant action. He wanted to land with a party at once and burn the vessels before the Tripolitans could make them secure. Morris on the quarterdeck of the *New York* eyed the shoals through his telescope—on that treacherous coast his frigates had to lie some miles from the shore—and could not make up his mind. Evening was at hand and he thought it might be better to wait until next day.

During the night the Tripolitan army arrived, and worked like beavers building fortifications out of the sacks of grain from the cargoes. Too late, Morris next morning sent in his boats with Porter in command. A dozen lives were uselessly thrown away. Porter fell wounded. The members of the landing party could not maintain themselves on the beach under the musketry fire from the defenses, and the enemy ships lay too far out for the Americans' gunfire to be effective. Morris transferred his attention from the coasters to the gunboats in Tripoli harbor. He made a feeble thrust at them, and failed again.

It was then, after two failures, that Morris decided to try for peace. He landed under a flag of truce, and the delighted Tripolitans witnessed the spectacle of an American captain, twice repulsed, now offering money to buy a treaty. They could only believe that Morris was moved by fear—there could be no other explanation possible in their minds. Even for us it is hard to understand how Morris could have made such a move; he must have been one of the weakest negotiators that ever was entrusted with American interests.

Congress had authorized Morris to pay up to twenty thousand dollars to secure peace in the Mediterranean. Because he had yet to make treaties with the other Barbary States, he could only offer five thousand dollars to Tripoli. What Tripoli thought of this offer soon became evident. She demanded no less than two hundred thousand dollars in cash and, in addition, repayment of every penny the war had cost her. This demand, if agreed to, gave promise of assuring Tripoli a steady income for years to come.

Morris was utterly crushed by the new failure. He sailed off to Malta again, leaving Rodgers in charge of the blockade. And it was not long before Rodgers had an opportunity to show what stuff he was made of. He kept close in to the port, close enough to notice any unusual movements there. His vigilance was rewarded. Quick eyes at the masthead of the *John Adams* saw the gunboats making preparations for going to sea. Rodgers alerted his three ships and spread them out to bar any possible move. The next morning at dawn he discovered a strange vessel running for Tripoli—she had mistimed her attempt to get in under cover of night.

There was instant action. The *Enterprise* cut the ship off from Tripoli, and she took refuge in a small bay fifteen miles away. Rodgers raced down to the attack. At the same moment the Tripolitan gunboats tried to work their way through the shoals to help their compatriot, and the Tripolitan army marched out hotfoot to play their part.

Rodgers did not waste a moment. Less than three hours after the Tripolitan ship was sighted, the *John Adams* opened fire on her. In that time Rodgers had sailed fifteen miles, worked his ship into the dangerous shoals, and was ready to anchor with "springs" on his cables. This was an arrangement by which he could turn his ship this way and that so as to direct his fire where he wished.

Now the heavy broadside guns of the *John Adams* began to pound the Tripolitan ship, and the latter returned the fire. Cannon smoke drifted around the bay as Rodgers, forbearing to anchor, worked in closer and closer. The well-directed fire was more than the Tripolitans could stand. They hoisted out their boats and fled ashore. At the same moment, the *John Adams,* in danger from rocks and shoals, had to head out again before she could send in her boats to capture the prize.

The Tripolitans started to come back on board their own ship. The Tripolitan army was fast approaching. Rodgers, seeing there was no time to lose, swung the *John Adams* around again and re-opened fire. The cannon shot tore through the ship, and a moment later the Americans were treated to a remarkable display as the Tripolitan ship blew up. Her masts flew a hundred and fifty feet straight up into the air out of the cloud of smoke that engulfed her. When the smoke cleared away there were only fragments floating among the rocks. This was less than four hours after the Tripolitan ship had been sighted. The gunboats hurried back to port, and the army turned around and marched home again.

It had been a brilliant action, well calculated to convince the Tripolitans of the American seamanship and fighting capacity. Now was the moment to press the attack upon the town and compel peace. And this was the moment when Morris's anxieties overcame him. There were no new ones; just the same old troubles of provisions and water, of enlistments expiring and Morocco threatening trouble. He had not even the weather to blame, for this was not yet the end of June, and he could look forward to more than two months of good weather. And yet he abandoned the blockade and sailed away with his squadron on a circular tour of the Western Mediterranean.

The only explanation that can be offered is that Morris found himself unable to support any longer the burden of his responsibilities. He may have been in such a mood that he could persuade himself that he had accomplished his task, or he may have thought that the task was one that could never be accomplished.

Off he went, through the lovely Straits of Messina, into the beautiful Bay of Naples. He conferred with the Minister of the King of Naples regarding the loan of small craft, and the possibility of using Neapolitan dockyards. The Neapolitan government was probably the most corrupt and inefficient in Europe, but its help might be better than nothing. That help was not offered very readily, because Naples was hesitating on the brink of entering into the war on one side or the other.

From Naples Morris proceeded slowly toward Gibraltar. When he was nearly there he received an order from the Secretary of the Navy removing him from his command. Morris was one of the few men who was at all surprised at such an action. His unhappy story ends with a court of inquiry and his dismissal from the Navy. It was a severe sentence, in fact a brutal one, especially as he had no opportunity of excusing himself before a court-martial. He paid, in fact, for the disappointment of the high hopes with which America had sent him out eighteen months before. Perhaps the severity of his treatment was a hint of the determination of the administration to fight the war with new energy.

CHAPTER 5

PHILADELPHIA AGROUND—307 PRISONERS TAKEN

MR. JEFFERSON AND THE SECRETARY OF THE Navy, Mr. Robert Smith, were indeed set on fighting to a finish. Man of peace though Jefferson was, and even though the cost of the war was appalling to his frugal mind, he was determined to go ahead. Morris's complaints about the lack of small craft resulted in Congress's voting the sum of ninety-six thousand dollars to build two schooners and two brigs. These were the famous ships the *Nautilus* and the *Vixen,* the *Argus* and the *Syren.*

The United States government was now acting vigorously. It might be thought that the Louisiana Purchase, which had just been completed, had given the nation new life. Now that her destiny of expansion was settled, the United States was determined to take her rightful place among the nations of the world.

Ships were being refitted, new crews were being recruited, and, most important of all, a new commander had been selected. Edward Preble was one of the most junior captains, a fact which caused constant trouble.

Seniority meant much in the United States Navy, as in all fighting services. In war one man can give orders to another which will send that man into deadly peril, perhaps to his death. And those orders are given by virtue of the fact that one man's commission bears a date perhaps only a few days earlier than the other's. Those orders are given, too, in the certainty of instant obedience; disobedience (although the fact is rarely mentioned) may be paid for by a shameful death before an execution squad. So seniority is of vast importance. Moreover, every officer of a fighting service who is worth

65

his salt is burning to distinguish himself. He will resent bitterly the appointment of a man junior to himself to a position that he might have had himself.

So seniority is not a matter to be treated lightly. No country has ever found it easy to put a senior under a junior's orders. Yet every country has to face the problem that an officer may be promoted and acquire seniority before there has been a chance to find out whether he is fit for high command.

The large navies of other countries solved this problem by promoting every captain in his turn to admiral and then leaving the unsatisfactory admirals unemployed or giving them administrative posts where they could do no harm. But America had no admirals (the title sounded undemocratic) and few enough captains, and administrative posts of any dignity did not exist.

The appointment of Preble to the command in the Mediterranean meant the recall of every captain senior to him, including the active and brilliant Rodgers. It also meant, that when the Mediterranean squadron was reinforced to the point where more captains were needed than there were captains junior to Preble, Preble had to give up the command. It was the price that had to be paid for discipline and order, and even Jefferson's genius could not devise a way around the difficulty.

After the removal of Morris, however, Preble was in command. He sailed in August, 1803, in the *Constitution,* arrived at Gibraltar in September, and made his personality and ability instantly felt throughout the squadron. So far, he was almost unknown to his brother officers, except by reputation as the man who in command of the *Essex* had sailed to Batavia and back without losing a single man from sickness. He had convoyed on that occasion an American merchant fleet halfway round the world to the romantic Spice Islands. His success had made him known among merchant skippers, but not among his brother captains, for he had been out of all contact with them for a year. But they soon learned to know him better, with his stern but just discipline, his abounding energy, his capacity for organization, and his fearless acceptance of responsibility. The peppery-tempered unknown soon became the beloved commander, and the American squadron at once became a force to be feared. Preble was like a skilled teamster taking over the reins after a clumsy driver had unsettled the horses; he had his team at once in hand and pulling vigorously and together.

And credit must be given to Jefferson and Robert Smith. It was they who had named Preble to the command; it was they who issued his orders, and it was they who chiefly selected the brilliant band of young officers who served under him. The victories of 1812 were mostly won by men who had been trained by Preble. Yet many of those men were first selected and put in the way of distinction by Mr. Robert Smith during Mr. Jefferson's administration.

The arrival of Preble and his ships brought an instant change in the North African situation. He struck at once at the nearest enemy. The Emperor of Morocco arrived at Tangier to find a powerful American squadron anchored in the port, their decks cleared for action and guns run out. The Moroccan ships of war were in American hands, their officers and crews were American prisoners, and it only needed a word from Preble to lay Tangier in ruins.

Preble had seized the right moment and the perfect opportunity to bring pressure on Morocco. Tangier was the most vulnerable of all the North African ports and Preble had the largest possible force in hand.

The Emperor had to yield at once, and there was a rapid change from war to peace, from hatred to friendship. The United States had never had such a good friend as the Empire of Morocco, declared the Emperor. The Moorish warships which had gone out to take prizes (and had fallen into American hands) had not been obeying his orders, but those of the Governor of Tangier, who would be punished for his behavior. The American ships must need fresh provisions. Here were live cattle and sheep and fowls, as a gift, not for sale. Surely now it would be easy to come to terms?

Easy enough, Preble replied, as long as those terms were his own. He demanded an instant declaration of peace with not a penny paid for it. There would not even be a present for the prime minister. Preble also demanded a mutual exchange of prisoners and prizes.

The Emperor agreed; the American prisoners were released, and the Moroccan vessels handed back. Peace was solemnly declared and salutes given and returned to ratify it. Now Preble could sail away with his free livestock on board.

There was still work to be done at the Gibraltar end of the Mediterranean. There were American ships to be convoyed. The blockade of Tripoli had to be reproclaimed to undo the work of Morris, one of whose last acts had been (yielding to Moroccan threats) to permit grain vessels free entry to Tripoli. Arrangements had to be made for American storeships to come far up the Mediterranean instead of stopping at Gibraltar as their previous contracts had agreed. But none of this was to delay for a moment the new blockade of Tripoli. Captain William Bainbridge had already been sent with the *Philadelphia* and *Vixen* to take station outside that port.

Preble dealt with his numerous affairs, established his line of communication, and started after him.

Then, early one morning, with the mountains of Sardinia in sight, the topsails of a frigate came up over the horizon. She was British—H.M.S. *Amazon*—and she sent up a signal to say that she had important news. It was appalling news.

The *Amazon* had just come from Malta. Before she left, the Danish consul there had received a letter from the Danish consul at Tripoli, telling that the *Philadelphia* had been captured. Bainbridge and three hundred and seven officers and men, and a fine frigate, were in the hands of the Tripolitan pirates. It was "melancholy and distressing intelligence," as Preble said in his report. He pushed on to Malta to hear the details, and Bainbridge's report awaited him there.

It was one of those disasters made possible only by a whole series of coincidences. Bainbridge, from his station off Tripoli, had sent the *Vixen* westward to intercept two corsairs that he had heard were cruising in that direction. Alone, he maintained the blockade until a westerly gale blew him away from the port. When the wind shifted and he was returning, he sighted a Tripolitan ship which was sneaking into the harbor. Bainbridge hurried to the attack, pressing in among the dangerous and unknown shallows, his guns firing at long range. From little platforms at the sides of the ship, he had men heaving the lead, constantly lowering over the side weights attached to lines by which they could tell the depths of water under the ship.

The Tripolitan ship had too good a start. She slipped into the harbor just in time and Bainbridge turned away, having penetrated to the very mouth of the harbor. The minarets and towers of Tripoli were plainly in view under the noontime sun. At that moment Lieutenant David Porter (newly recovered from his wounds) was by Bainbridge's orders climbing the rigging of the mizzen mast so as to be able to see what other ships the Tripolitans had in harbor, and in what state of readiness.

The lead was hauled up ready to be cast again. Before it could drop—before Porter could reach the masthead—

there was a shattering crash and a mighty jerk as the *Philadelphia* reared up and stopped, her bows inclined upwards, and leaning heavily over to one side. The *Philadelphia* was fast aground on the Kaliusa reef, well known of course to the Tripolitans but not marked on any chart that Bainbridge had. He had taken every possible precaution he could without being timid, and this disaster had befallen him.

He did all he could to get his ship free. He turned his sails against the wind in an attempt to back the ship off the rocks. He set his men to work in furious haste on the heeling deck to lighten her so that she might float. Everything was flung over the side: the anchors and then the guns, save for one or two that might be used to defend the ship against attack. The pumps were set to work, pumping the precious drinking water into the sea.

It was of no use; the bow had run too far up onto the rocks—she lay there in only twelve feet of water. There was one last sacrifice that could be made. Axes were brought and the shrouds that supported the foremast were cut. As soon as they parted the mast fell over the side, so greatly was the ship heeled over. The foremast was of great weight, and of course losing it relieved the ship in the part that was most aground, but the loss did not set her free. She was still hard and fast on the rocks, and nothing, it seemed, would float her off.

Nor was all this work performed without interference. The delighted Tripolitans, as soon as they saw what had happened, manned their gunboats and swarmed out to the attack. They were only little boats, but that meant they could be easily moved with oars. The one or two guns they carried were very heavy and powerful, capable of sending a shot through the side of any ship in the world. The Tripolitans came rowing out across the harbor, clustered under the stern of the helpless ship, and opened a slow but methodical fire.

Bainbridge could do nothing in reply. His ship had fallen so far over on one side, and the bows were forced so high, that he could not use the guns he had left, especially as the Tripolitans chose to attack on the quarter. This was the angle between the stern and the side, where ships of that day, even when on an even keel, found difficulty in bringing guns into action. Bainbridge hauled a gun or two to the threatened point, and had his men bring their axes there and actually cut away part of the side of the ship to try to return the fire. He found, however, that this was impossible on a deck that pointed to the sky.

It was part of Bainbridge's bad luck that he had sent the *Vixen* away. Had she been with him she would probably have been used in the chase, and the *Philadelphia* would not have gone aground at all. Even with the *Philadelphia* aground, the *Vixen* would have kept the gunboats at a distance and prevented any attack from the shore, so that Bainbridge could have floated his ship off. As it was, he had no chance.

The gunboats continued their monotonous pounding. For six hours the men had toiled without success to free the ship, and darkness was approaching. But not darkness only. The Tripolitan army of several thousand men was ready by now. There were scores of small boats available to carry them out to the wreck, and the few guns left would not be able to fire on them. In the darkness an attack would be launched with odds of ten to one, and there would be massacre and murder.

Bainbridge fulfilled his last duty. The pumps were set to work again, pumping water onto the gunpowder in the magazines. Everything that might be of value to a warlike power—the muskets, the cutlasses—was thrown overboard, and the carpenter was sent down to bore holes in the bottom of the ship. And then, just after the flaming sun had set, and as the attack gathered strength, Bainbridge hauled down the flag.

The Tripolitans swarmed on board, mad as usual for personal plunder. They stripped the wretched prisoners of their clothes before bringing them ashore. There was a surf breaking on the beach and the Americans were forced to wade in through it, to where the Tripolitan army was waiting for them. Then the Americans were marched to their prison—a dirty warehouse which they had to clean out before it was fit for habitation, and so small that there was not floor space for them all to lie down at once. Not until the evening of the next day did anyone think of giving them anything to eat.

Bainbridge and his officers were led in triumph through the marble halls of the palace, before the Pasha on his throne, and then confined in the house which until a short time before had been occupied by the American consul.

But there was much more to add to their unhappiness. Two days after the surrender a brisk wind came blowing in from the sea. It piled the water up on the reef to increase the depth, and helped the thousands of men who were set to work to recover the ship. Anchors were laid out astern of her with cables leading to the ship, and the Tripolitans labored at the capstan to haul her off. The gunboats pulled with all the strength of their rowers, and eventually the *Philadelphia* came free.

In a sheltered harbor, with plenty of skilled labor at hand, the leaks in the vessel's bottom could be easily dealt with. Tripoli now had in her possession the finest frigate she had ever owned, built by Josiah Fox to the order of the city after which she was named, as a gift to the United States.

Nor was that all. The guns and weapons which Bainbridge had thrown overboard lay on the rocks in less than twenty feet of water. There were plenty of coral divers and sponge fishers in Tripoli to whom twenty feet of water was a trifle. It was not long before the guns were mounted again on the *Philadelphia* and the ship was once more a dangerous fighting vessel. The prisoners, when they were marched to work on the fortifications, could look out unhappily across the harbor and see the *Philadelphia* riding to her anchor with the Tripolitan flag at her peak.

It was a state of affairs that enormously complicated Preble's task. He was under orders not only to make war on Tripoli but also to negotiate a peace. And now Tripoli had in her possession bargaining counters of great value. No doubt the pirates would put up their price. They had won a decided victory, and, even though luck had given it to them, it was only natural that they might think they could win others. It was possible that they might, by actual ill-treatment of the prisoners, put pressure on Preble to hasten the conclusion of peace. Even if they did not do so deliberately it was not pleasant for Preble to think about the three hundred Americans in enemy hands.

It was usual, in those days, for a nation to give the prisoners that it took the same rations and treatment that it gave its own fighting men. (Later on the practice became the subject of treaties between various countries.) But the Tripolitan seaman was never properly fed or clothed by his government, so that Bainbridge's men could expect to be starved and cold and verminous, as indeed they were. Preble knew that should he refuse the terms demanded by Tripoli he was prolonging and perhaps increasing the misery suffered by his fellow countrymen.

The capture of the *Philadelphia* introduced another complication, for it gave the pirates a vessel of speed and power. There was always the chance that they might man her and bring her out to fight, and in all Preble's squadron there was only the *Constitution* that could hope to meet her with any chance of success. It was a possibility that always had to be borne in mind; one more anxiety for Preble.

He dealt with his problems without any delay. He found food and water for his ships. Through the British consul he was able to send money and clothing to Bainbridge for the use of the prisoners. He re-rigged the *Syren,* for the shipbuilders in the yard had tried to improve on her design and had injured her sailing qualities thereby. He made an inquiry of the Tripolitan agent at Malta regarding peace terms, and sheered off abruptly when he heard that the first item was a demand by Tripoli for a complete schooner of war in exchange for the *Philadelphia.*

Preble went down to Tripoli with his squadron and for the first time in his life he examined the place with his own eyes. It was probably then that he began to form the plan that he carried out so brilliantly shortly afterwards. And of course he tightened up the blockade of the port, weathering the winter gales and capturing, to the vast annoyance of the Pasha, the ketch *Mastico,* a small two-masted sailing ship. It was carrying presents—among them forty-two African slaves—for the Ottoman government at Constantinople.

Here was one of the small craft so urgently needed for inshore fighting. Preble took the *Mastico* into the American service. He had to give her a new name. No one knows now just why he selected the name *Intrepid,* but whether the choice was casual or not it added a glorious name to the records of American naval history.

CHAPTER 6

DECATUR DESTROYS THE *PHILADELPHIA*

PREBLE WAS ALREADY RESOLVED THAT THE *Philadelphia* must be destroyed. Probably he had decided on that as soon as he heard the news of her loss, before even he gazed at her through his telescope as the *Constitution* beat about outside the harbor. He had only to decide upon a plan of action, one that had a chance of success, at whatever cost.

Bainbridge, in prison, had written to him in invisible ink suggesting such an attempt. Now Stephen Decatur, who had been sent back to the Mediterranean and was captain of the *Enterprise,* came to him with suggestions.

And immediately afterwards, Lieutenant Charles Stewart, commanding the *Syren,* also asked for an interview and proposed an attack on the *Philadelphia.* It was only natural that every officer and man in the squadron should wish to redeem her loss.

The ideal, of course, would be to recapture her, bring her out from Tripoli and hoist the Stars and Stripes once more on board her. In naval history there were plenty of examples of similar feats, and during the then current war between France and England new ones were being continually added. The usual plan was to send in a large attacking force by night in boats, to board the vessel, overpower her crew, and come sailing out with the prize. Preble must have thought longingly of doing the same, and yet he rejected the scheme. There might be three hundred, there might be five hundred, men on board the *Philadelphia,* and the total number of men under his own command was less than a thousand. It would be hard to send in a force that could be certain of seizing the *Philadelphia* and at the same time retain enough men to man his own ships adequately.

Besides, a force of three hundred men would fill seven or eight boats, and seven or eight boats could not hope to escape detection while rowing all the way up into Tripoli harbor. An alarm, an early warning to the *Philadelphia,* would deprive the boarding party of the advantage of

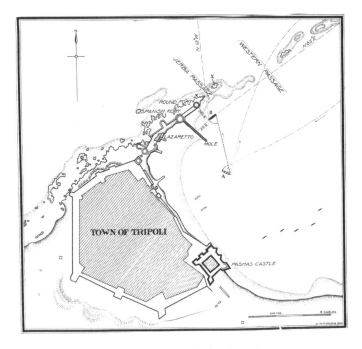

Historical Chart of Tripoli Harbor

"A" marks Philadelphia's *position when boarded by Decatur's men from the* Intrepid, *16 February, 1804.*

"B" is the location of her wreck.

"X" (just west of the Jerba Passage) is the location of the Intrepid's *wreck after she blew up on 4 September 1804, during another mission into Tripoli harbor.*

surprise and would result in a long fight. That could bring about both the arrival of reinforcements from the Tripolitan army on shore and also the battering by the guns of the defenses of the ship if captured.

Preble saw clearly that the attempt must not fail. Another defeat, another repulse, would mean that negotiations with Tripoli for any reasonable terms of peace would be impossible. It might also have a depressing effect on his own forces, although now that Preble was coming to know the young men under his command he thought he could put that fear aside.

But it was a long, long way out to the gap in the reef from where the *Philadelphia* lay at anchor. A wind that would carry an attacking force in would work against them when they tried to sail the *Philadelphia* out. Furthermore, the Tripolitans had not yet replaced the foremast Bainbridge had cut away. Perhaps, thought Preble, his men could tow the *Philadelphia* out with boats. No, that would take a long time—a full hour. All that time the batteries could fire on the fragile boats towing, and the Tripolitan gunboats could cut them off.

No, there was too little hope of bringing the *Philadelphia* out, and this was not the moment to take a very big risk. Preble, sitting in his cabin or walking his quarterdeck—already tortured by the disease that was to kill him a few years later—had to discard the idea.

So if the *Philadelphia* could not be brought out she must be destroyed. That would be risky enough, but it was a risk worth taking. That meant setting her on fire— wooden ships were hard to sink but easy to burn. The timbers were weathered and covered with paint; the rigging was tarred—flame would run up a burning rope like a firework. The sails were great masses of dry canvas, and then there was the powder magazine; it would take only a single spark there to blow the ship to fragments. Fire was the most constant danger in the old ships, and strict rules were enforced about lights on board. If a determined body of men set the *Philadelphia* thoroughly on fire she was doomed.

But it could only be a small body of men; that was already plain, for it was absolutely necessary to achieve surprise. Those men must get on board without causing an alarm to be given. It could be done by use of clever disguise. The thought of disguise called to Preble's mind the captured *Mastico*—the new *Intrepid*. There she was, looking like all the hundreds of other small coasters to be found in the inlets of North Africa. She might come in unquestioned, sneaking in at night like any other blockade runner. Then she could drift alongside the *Philadelphia,* and determined men could do the rest. There would be other advantages in using the *Intrepid*. She was small enough to be moved by oars—the long sweeps that every North African craft employed—so that she could get out again without depending on the wind. That would give her crew at least a chance of escape. Preble of course did not want his men to lose their lives, nor did he want to see another batch of captives added to the three hundred that Tripoli already held prisoner. But being small, the *Intrepid* could carry only a small force. Preble called in Decatur and discussed the question again.

Decatur undertook the mission, naturally, eagerly. Stewart was disappointed. It was his hard luck that Decatur had had first opportunity of discussing the mission with Preble. That gave Decatur the right to try it, together with the opportunity of distinguishing himself, and the chance of being killed. Every man in Decatur's *Enterprise* volunteered. Decatur took sixty-two of them. Also included in the party were his own officers, five midshipmen from the *Constitution,* and—may his name be remembered—a Sicilian named Salvatore Catalano, who served with the squadron as pilot.

The *Intrepid* was sixty feet long (there are plenty of pleasure yachts larger than that), and the seventy-four men crammed themselves on board. The *Constitution,* the *Intrepid,* the *Enterprise,* and the *Syren* were lying in Syracuse harbor in Sicily at the time, and there every man was drilled in the part he was to play. Every man knew what he had to do once the *Intrepid* was alongside the *Philadelphia*. Preble's written orders to Decatur went into great detail regarding exactly how the ship was to be set on fire. This was a sign of the anxiety Preble felt, as otherwise he would have left a free hand to that very capable officer, Decatur.

So off went the *Intrepid* with the *Syren* under Stewart's command to accompany her. The men on board were crammed so close that midshipmen and marines shared the privilege of sleeping on top of the water casks in the hold. They were packed like sardines—and at the same time devoured by the vermin left in the ship by the former African owners. They ate the stores found in the ship, too, and the food was stinking and rotten. But it was only four days' easy sail from Syracuse to Tripoli, and they could endure four days of discomfort.

The night of their arrival a roaring westerly wind such as one might expect in February blew them far to the eastward. This forced the men to endure nine days more as they beat back to the harbor—nine days more of cramp and suffocation, vermin and food poisoning. At last they crawled back to Tripoli, and sighted the place with a gentle northerly wind blowing. The *Intrepid* took the lead, and the *Syren* held back so as not to appear to be acquainted.

The Americans looking out from their prison saw the two vessels and wondered what they were. The *Syren* was far distant, and no one recognized her; what with the convoy work she had undertaken and the alterations carried out in Malta, she was unknown at Tripoli. The *Intrepid* was obviously a merchant ship, and William Ray, the captured marine whose diary tells us much about what went on in Tripoli, thought that she might be bringing in envoys to discuss peace. What he did not know, and what Preble's intelligence service had discovered, was that the Tripolitans had recently bought at Malta a two-masted vessel rigged like the *Syren,* and were expecting her arrival.

The wind was dropping now and night was approaching. It had been agreed in the original plan that the *Intrepid* was to be reinforced by the boats and boats' crews of the *Syren,* but Decatur decided that he would not wait for them. By a fortunate chance he had taken over one of the *Syren's* boats the day before, and it was towing astern. His timing was excellent. Without appearing to delay, he had reached the entrance to the harbor just after nightfall, and by the light of the moon he was able to steer for the *Philadelphia*.

He and Catalano and one or two more were visible on deck wearing Turkish clothing; the others were lying out of sight, flat on the deck or huddled in the hold. The wind carried the boat ever so slowly toward the *Philadelphia,* with Catalano steering.

The Tripolitan crew were taking the evening air on deck, idly watching the *Intrepid* approaching. They hailed to warn her to keep clear, but Catalano hailed back in *lingua franca,* the mixture of all the languages spoken round the Mediterranean. A Turk would use it when speaking to a Berber.

Catalano was ready with his story—it had long been thought out. He said his ship had lost her anchors, and asked permission to tie up alongside the *Philadelphia* for the night. Permission was granted without a thought, and a word or two of gossip exchanged. Catalano's statement that the brig outside was the *Transfer*—that was the name of the brig which the Tripolitans had just bought at Malta—gave the final touch of reality.

When the two vessels were only twenty yards apart, the wind failed. This left the *Intrepid* lying helpless, with the seventy men of her crew hardly daring to breathe as they lay tightly packed on the planking. As in any other military plan, however well devised, something unexpected had happened, and bold action, clear-headed action, was necessary. At a murmured order from Decatur, the men in Turkish dress climbed down into the *Syren's* boat, which was mercifully towing astern. Slowly and leisurely it had to be done, however desperate the moment, because haste and smartness would be suspicious.

By the time the Americans had taken a rope from the *Intrepid's* bow, the *Philadelphia* had obligingly sent off her boat with a rope too. After the two ropes were fastened together, the boats returned to their respective ships. The men in sight on the deck began to haul in on the rope; those lying down seized it and gave what help they could. Then the *Intrepid* began to close the gap between the ships, inch by inch and yard by yard. The sides of the vessels were about to touch when a cry of alarm went up from the *Philadelphia*.

"Board!" said Decatur, and the Americans sprang to their feet, weapons in hand, and clambered up the side of the *Philadelphia*. It was a complete surprise; not one Tripolitan had time to seize musket or pistol as the wave of Americans swept along the decks. Not a shot was fired. One American received a wound; a score of Tripolitans who tried to show fight or who were too stupefied to run were cut down.

Decatur led the final charge on the Tripolitans huddled together in the bows. He swept them overboard—into the sea or down into their boat.

Already the rest of the plan was under way. The Americans who had been detailed to remain in the *Intrepid* were passing out oily rags, bundles of straw and oakum soaked in turpentine—everything for a quick, fierce blaze. The boarding parties took them and hurried them to the cockpit and the storerooms and the berth deck.

The glowing slow matches were whirled round until they were burning brightly, and then were thrust into the heaps.

In the cramped quarters of a wooden ship a heap of straw blazing on one deck would have the deck above on fire in a moment; with the hatchways and ports all open there was plenty of draft. It was scarcely a matter of seconds before the whole ship was full of roaring flames. So quickly did they spread that one or two Americans were nearly cut off by them. But everyone succeeded in tumbling back on board—they even dragged back with them one unhappy Tripolitan prisoner. Then they cut the ropes and shoved the *Intrepid* clear.

There was desperate need for haste because on the *Intrepid*'s deck were plenty more combustibles, piled there in case Decatur should see an opportunity of using the *Intrepid* as a fireship. A spark from the blazing inferno which the *Philadelphia* had become would send the *Intrepid* up in flames as well. This was not a time for further risks, so the crew, remembering their drill, began to row the *Intrepid* away. Although they worked hard, with long, long pulls at the clumsy oars, their movements seemed painfully slow, but the *Intrepid* gradually gathered way.

It took time to cover any distance. Luckily, it also took time for the Tripolitans to come to their senses, for the sleeping garrison on shore to wake up and get to their guns, for the crews of the other ships to hoist up their anchors. Most of the firing came from the *Philadelphia's* own guns, which were loaded and went off one by one as the flames reached them. The flames were already roaring up the rigging. They reached the cables that secured the vessel and burned them through, so that the frigate for a little while drifted in the harbor.

At last the fire reached the magazine and the explosion blew the ship to fragments, which rained down into the harbor. Some of the fragments were dredged up from the bottom forty years later by an American captain.

Stewart, in the *Syren* outside the harbor, saw the blaze and knew that the attack had gained its objective. He saw the explosion, and then, long minutes afterwards, he saw the rocket which Decatur sent up. It announced that the *Intrepid* had escaped and gave notice of her location. Stewart sent in his boats to help her, and soon Decatur stepped on board the *Syren* to report to his superior.

It was not for long that Stewart would be Decatur's superior, for Decatur was promoted to captain over Stewart's head as soon as the news of the *Philadelphia's* destruction reached America. That was the fortune of war, and Stewart had to be content with promotion to the rank of Master Commandant, newly revived by Congress.

As if to make up for the tricks it had played previously, the wind now freshened and blew from the right quarter. It was only for three nights and two days that the seventy men in the *Intrepid* had to endure overcrowding and fleas and poisonous food.

Preble, waiting at Syracuse in the *Constitution*, with the *Vixen* and the *Enterprise* anchored beside him, saw the two ships coming up over the horizon, sixteen days after they had set out. We can only guess how long those sixteen days had seemed to Preble. The grim, lean old man, with what was left of his once red hair already gray, heard the news that his plan had been completely successful. Not a life had been lost, and there was nothing left of the *Philadelphia*.

CHAPTER 7

U.S. MAINTAINS FRAGILE BLOCKADE

THE BURNING OF THE *PHILADELPHIA* WAS A load off Preble's mind; but Preble's mind bore many loads. Although he was free now from the nightmare possibility of the Tripolitans sailing out in the *Philadelphia,* he still had plenty to think about. There was the blockade to be maintained, through the wild winter weather, and he maintained it, although storms damaged his ships and presented him with the fresh problem of how to get them repaired. That the blockade was effective was proved by the prizes that he took.

Yet those prizes meant more reports to be written and

more responsibility, for a blockade always brings about trouble with the neutrals whose business is being interfered with and whose property is being seized. Many times in her history America has been the neutral, and has naturally experienced a sense of grievance at her losses. At that very moment United States shipping was suffering because of the war between England and Napoleon. The same thing would happen again in 1916 when England would be at war with Germany.

Of course, the United States has felt differently when she has been the blockading power. During the Civil War the American Navy enforced the blockade of Southern ports as rigorously as any blockade has ever been enforced. And in 1917 when the United States declared war on Germany she tightened up the rules against which she had protested the year before.

The United States was the blockading power in 1806 in the Mediterranean, and Preble enforced her rights, seizing ships of any nationality that tried to run either inward or outward through the blockade he had proclaimed. He was fully entitled to do so, especially as he took care to maintain the blockade day after day. (By international law a blockade must be constant and maintained in force.) But the sufferers protested. Morocco and Tunis and Algiers neither liked the thought of their fellow Muslims being under blockade nor wished to lose the profits resulting from the transport of foodstuffs to Tripoli.

The owners of other captured ships protested to their governments and threatened to bring suit against Preble in the Federal Courts for damages. There was a Russian ship which Stewart caught trying to escape from Tripoli. Preble could have made a prize of her, but he let her go. He knew that the Czar of Russia was a man of uncertain temper who believed he had great interests in the Mediterranean. He laid claim to rule over Malta, and had a powerful fleet in the Mediterranean at that moment. Preble, rather than risk offending a freakish monarch who had seven battleships close at hand, gave up the prize. It must be remembered that under the old laws, Preble received a share of the value of every prize taken.

Giving up the Russian ship was a sensible act, but it meant more letters, reports and decisions.

Another source of trouble was the King of Naples, who had to be persuaded to lend gunboats and crews for the attack on Tripoli that Preble intended. The King, with his kingdom trembling on the brink of disaster (less than two years later Napoleon seized half his dominions), was a man who found it hard to make up his mind. Preble had to write many letters and use much persuasion to bring him to a decision.

Then there was the eternal question of food and water. Preble was at liberty to purchase stores from Sicily, but that was the most misgoverned corner of Europe (under the same King of Naples). And although it was hard to find stores there, it was harder still to meet the prices that were asked by the Sicilians during the wartime shortages. Stores sent out from America were at least two months old when they reached him, and we find Preble reporting that a large amount had to be thrown overboard as useless upon arrival.

To add to his troubles, the terms of enlistment of his men were expiring. That had to be attended to and more men found and trained. Of course, like every officer commanding any fleet anywhere in the world, he was plagued by the desertion of some of his seamen.

Life on board a ship of war was desperately hard, and when the opportunity came, many men tried to escape. This was especially true of those men who had incurred the dislike of some officer and who faced a future of repeated floggings. (It was 1861 before flogging was abolished in the United States Navy.) That being the case, it was better to escape even into another ship of war to start afresh. It was certainly better to escape into a merchant ship where the pay was far higher and conditions not so severe.

Seamen in general were literally a floating population, with no home ties, and no families. They spent their hard brief lives in one ship after another, quite unfitted for any life on shore. It hardly mattered to them which country they served or under which flag they sailed. So American seamen deserted to British ships, and British seamen deserted to American ships. This was, of course, trouble-some to the captains who lost their services and had to try to replace them.

Preble made use of Sicilian ports rather than British because of this very problem of desertion. In Sicily there were not so many ships to desert into and with most of his men the difference of language discouraged deser-tion to the shore. It meant trouble one way or the other in any case.

CHAPTER 8

PREBLE ATTACKS TRIPOLI!

UNDER THE BLUE SKY LAY THE VIVID COLORS of the Mediterranean. Far out the sea was a blue even more intense than the sky, but nearer in the blue abruptly changed to a clear green, and beyond that the green shaded into yellow, marking the shoals that made this coast so dangerous. A line of jagged rocks, gray and black and red, constituted more obvious dangers to ships venturing in.

On the far side of the rocks stretched the shore line, low and level, in color a yellowish sandy gray, but so low that for a little way out to sea it was invisible. Yet it could still be traced by the palm trees that extended along it, their feathery tops spaced out all along the horizon.

There was nothing remarkable about the coast except for the city that stood there, with the palms extending on either side of it. Gleaming white in the sunshine lay the city within its bastioned walls. Above it towered the castle, a hundred and fifty feet high, solidly built in its lower stories but arched and airy in the upper ones. From the flagstaff above it the flag of Tripoli fluttered in the gentle land breeze.

On that blazing afternoon the little harbor was a scene of furious activity. Cannons were roaring and booming in a continuous rolling of gunfire, and powder smoke was drifting in dense banks over the sea. Men were fighting desperately for their lives and honor amid the shafts of sunlight that pierced the powder smoke.

Commodore Preble was delivering his attack upon Tripoli. There was to be an end of simple blockade, of negotiations, and of threats. Vigorous action might bring the pirates to their senses. Preble had assembled every ship and every man available for this assault, but the sum total of ships and men was neither great nor terrifying. Of ships there were a single frigate, half a dozen little brigs and schooners no bigger than a wealthy man's yacht, and eight clumsy gun vessels that were smaller still. The total of all the crews was only a thousand men, and of these a hundred were Neapolitans borrowed from the King of Naples to help man the borrowed gun vessels.

To oppose this small force, Tripoli had her light craft with nearly as many men as Preble had under his command, and she had manned her shore batteries of a hundred heavy guns with thousands of gunners. Preble was embarking upon a desperate venture in attempting to take wooden ships in against those stone walls, and amid those rocks and shoals. However, if skill and courage could gain a victory in the face of such odds, the skill and courage were available. The list of the junior officers is studded with names destined for immortality. Decatur and Stewart, James Lawrence and Thomas Macdonough were only a few among the many young and vigorous men burning for distinction and reckless of their lives.

Stephen Decatur took his division of three gunboats in among the Tripolitan light vessels where they sheltered among the shoals. Outnumbered in boats and vastly outnumbered in men, he attacked with a dash and ferocity that the Barbary pirates could not match. He took his own gunboat alongside a Tripolitan and boarded her. Sixteen men followed him with ax and pike, pistol and cutlass. There were thirty-six of the enemy, but the wild attack gave them no chance. Sixteen were killed and fifteen wounded before the remaining five had time to surrender.

Decatur was towing the Tripolitan vessel away as a prize when he heard that his brother had just been mortally wounded by a pirate who had pretended to surrender. The news helped to keep his fighting fury at a white heat. A moment later he was alongside another Tripolitan gunboat—whether the assassin's or not, no one can be sure—and a moment after that, he was leaping on her deck with Macdonough and the remnant of his crew following him. There were twenty-four Tripolitans to oppose him, headed by their burly captain. Decatur's cutlass broke off at the hilt when it clashed against the Tripolitan's pike. Undaunted, Decatur grappled and fell with his man, and shot him with a pistol which he did not draw from his pocket but fired through the cloth of his coat. The raging Americans then went storming on into the crowded boat. Three unwounded Tripolitans surrendered; four more were wounded but lived, and the other seventeen were dead.

Decatur brought out his two prizes; Lieutenant John Trippe had brought out another.

Meanwhile Preble had come boldly in with the *Constitution,* tacking and weaving so that his guns could sweep every part of the Tripolitan defenses in turn. The batteries he fired at promptly ceased their fire as the gunners ducked behind cover, and as promptly opened fire again as he turned away. Preble's grapeshot swept away the crews of some of the gunboats. These men were promptly replaced from the waiting hundreds on shore. But his round-shot sank two or three of the gunboats.

Meanwhile his two "mortar vessels" had been trying to throw shells into the city. The "mortar vessels" were Neapolitan ships, with Neapolitan shells, and not very effective. The shells scared most of the civilian population out into the surrounding country, and damaged a good many houses, including that of the Danish consul—an innocent bystander if ever there was one.

So the sultry afternoon wore on—an afternoon in Africa in August, with the cannon thundering over the water and the great banks of powder smoke drifting in the slight breeze. But there was a special significance about the drifting of that smoke. It was beginning to blow into shore. The wind was veering around, blowing from sea to land, as is always likely to happen in hot latitudes in the afternoon. Every moment made it more difficult to keep the wind from sweeping the American sailing ships toward that dangerous shore. If a ship should be disabled the task would be nearly impossible—

and already the *Constitution* had one shot clean through her mainmast.

Preble hoisted the signal that told his small fleet to leave the scene of action. As he swung his ship around he let loose with a couple of final broadsides. They brought down the minaret of the mosque, a Muslim house of prayer and worship that towered beside the castle.

The little squadron worked its way clear, prizes and all, and gathered round the flagship out at sea. But there could be no question of resting. Every officer and man fell to work preparing for a new attack, urged on not only by Preble's orders but by his own desire to give the enemy no time to recover. All the ships were much cut about in their rigging; new sails had to be bent and new ropes rove. The three prizes were re-rigged completely and crews allotted to them. Ammunition and provisions had to be distributed.

The work was finished in less than forty-eight hours. Then in went the squadron again, cannon thundering, officers walking the decks with the enemy's shot howling overhead, gun crews toiling in the heat with tackles and rammers, and powder boys running about with cartridges.

The enemy had learned from experience. This time more of their light craft came to grips with the Americans, and the guns were better aimed. Probably the Pasha of Tripoli (the Bashaw, as Preble spelt his title, with a much better attempt at the pronunciation) had been threatening to take off a few heads if more damage were not done to the enemy. The American gunboats were badly battered and one of them blew up. After three hours of furious fighting Preble drew off again as the wind worked around.

That night he received crushing news. The frigate *John Adams* had arrived while the action was at its height. She was not of much use as a reinforcement, for most of her guns were unmounted to make room for the stores she carried. Far worse, she carried dispatches to say that Preble was being superseded in his command. Commodore Samuel Barron was on his way with four additional frigates; and as there were only two more

111

captains on the Navy List junior to Preble, the command had to be given to an officer senior to him. It was a bitter blow to Preble, who had been in command for a whole year in the Mediterranean, bearing heavy responsibilities and struggling against endless difficulties.

Nor was this all—not by any means. Preble had no way of knowing when Barron would arrive, and meanwhile the summer was coming to an end. This was August, and by September bad weather might be expected, with northerly gales that would make the coast even more dangerous. It was Preble's duty to shoulder the responsibility and press on with the attack while the good weather lasted. At the same time, he knew that if he failed he would receive all the blame. If he were to succeed, the credit would be given to Barron. Yet the difficulties were mounting. Drinking water was running short, as always in ships that carried their supplies in wooden barrels. Some of the water had been five months in the casks, in a hot climate. Even so, it was necessary to put an armed sentry over the water to prevent the thirsty men from drinking all they wanted.

In addition, scurvy was making its appearance among the men—the horrible disease that rotted men's jaws and covered their bodies with sores. Scurvy was to be expected in ships that had been long at sea with the men fed only on salted meat and dry biscuit. We know now that it is caused by the absence of Vitamin C. Preble was aware that fresh vegetables would cure it, and he had to turn aside from his task of planning the next attack to make arrangements to obtain vegetables along with fresh water.

A greater problem was that the ships themselves were wearing out as a result of continuous service. Ropes and canvas were becoming worn, in addition to the damage done by the enemy's fire. The *John Adams* had brought fresh supplies of needed goods, but they had to be transferred at sea, with the ships rolling and tossing in the stormy Mediterranean.

Preble faced his difficulties without flinching, re-equipped his ships, sent to Sicily for water and vegetables, and went in again and again to the attack. He tried everything that his active, clever mind could suggest. He made night attacks, for he knew that not only would the shore batteries find it harder to aim in the darkness, but the population would resent having to spend sleepless nights while the bomb vessels were at work. He pressed his attack on the Tripolitan gunboats until the American light craft actually came under the fire of musketry from the shore. He took the *Constitution* boldly into the harbor to pour her fire into the castle and the batteries.

As the days passed and the weather grew more and more unfavorable he resolved on one last desperate stroke. He would send an explosion ship into the harbor. She would be filled with tons of gunpowder. A brave crew would take her in at night, right up against the city, would light the fuses, and try to escape. (Preble knew that there would be no lack of volunteers for any venture, however dangerous.) The explosion would destroy the shipping sheltering under the castle, and with luck would wreck the castle and unroof every house.

The vessel selected for the attempt was one with a long history, the ketch *Intrepid*. She had already played the leading part in one of the most glorious episodes in the campaign—the burning of the *Philadelphia*. Now she was to make another daring entrance into the Tripoli harbor.

Master-Commandant Richard Somers volunteered for the command. He was an old friend of Decatur's, and had been at school with him in Philadelphia. However, the fortunes of war and accidents of weather had prevented him from covering himself with glory as Decatur had succeeded in doing. Other officers and men volunteered for the service; more than one man contrived to get on board in defiance of orders.

Seven tons of gunpowder were jammed into the hold of the little vessel. Then to increase the violence of the explosion and to scatter further destruction, heaps of shells, scrap iron, and solid shot were placed on top of the gunpowder. There were masses of combustibles which the explosion might send, flaming, into the enemy's ships and magazines. After the powder trains were laid, the fuses were put into position.

At nine o'clock in the evening of September 4th, when it was pitch dark and a gentle wind was blowing conveniently into the harbor, the *Intrepid* was ready for action. Somers, Lieutenant Henry Wadsworth, his second in command, Lieutenant Joseph Israel, an officer who came without orders, and the ten or more brave men of his crew, took the ship in through the darkness. Her escort saw her go; then they saw the orange flashes of the Tripolitan guns piercing the night as they opened fire on the *Intrepid.*

Those aboard her escort had every hope that the *Intrepid* would be able to make her way through gunfire directed by men who were taken by surprise and blinded by their own gun flashes. But the hope was baseless, and the heroism and self-sacrifice of the thirteen volunteers were wasted. Something went wrong. Perhaps she was hit by a shot from the batteries. Perhaps a man—perhaps Somers himself—waiting with a light in his hand was hit and fell. Perhaps there was an accident, as well there might be in a ship full of explosives on a desperate mission and under hostile fire.

The watchers saw a great flash, too soon, far too soon, for the *Intrepid* to have reached her goal. The flash lit up the spars and rigging that were flung high into the air.

There was a fountain of exploding shells, and then there was darkness and silence. The thirteen men were dead. The *Intrepid* had blown up when she was barely through the gap in the reef, and the damage she had done to Tripoli was negligible.

Perhaps, some might say, it would have been better if the attempt had never been made, for the Tripolitans were emboldened by the knowledge that the Americans, for all their courage and ingenuity, had failed. Now the Tripolitans could await further attacks with a confidence that had been considerably weakened by the previous assaults.

Preble was of a mind to show them their error. The very day after the *Intrepid* exploded he ordered a fresh attack, but the weather turned unkind as usual, so the attack had to be called off. And the weather showed no signs of relenting. The unhandy gunboats and mortar vessels would be in grave danger on that rocky coast. Ammunition—especially after seven tons of gunpowder had been lost in the *Intrepid*—was running short. Men and material were wearing out. Preble had to decide to return to the old system of blockade, and he sent his light craft back to Sicily.

No sooner had he done so than Commodore Barron arrived at last with the frigates and the stores that would have been so useful a month earlier. There was no place for Preble in the new squadron. Already a sick man, he handed over his command, to the sorrow of everyone who had served under him. Before leaving, he gave Barron what help he could in maintaining good relations with the British at Malta and Gibraltar and with the Sicilians at Palermo and Syracuse. Then he sailed for home. Preble had not long to live; not long enough to see the officers he had trained attain the glory and distinction which was to be theirs in later years. It was under Preble that Decatur and Macdonough and many others acquired the habits of thought and the professional ability which won victories for them later on.

Preble (we know from his letters that he pronounced his name "Prebble") can be looked upon as the man who made the most important contribution to the founding of the United States Navy. He was hot-tempered and severe, but his subordinates loved him. He left the Mediterranean with Tripoli still a source of trouble, but he had trained an efficient navy. The example he set, customs he established, and the tradition that he began were to last long after his death. His genius for organization and his grasp of naval problems left their mark on all the subsequent history of the United States.

CHAPTER 9

JEFFERSON CONSIDERS LANDING TROOPS IN NORTH AFRICA

AFTER PREBLE'S DEPARTURE, BARRON TOOK over the task of reducing Tripoli to reason. Winter with its gales was close at hand; there could be no question of further attacks on the port, but the blockade could be maintained vigorously. There were repeated captures and several skirmishes when blockade runners tried to take refuge on the coast under the protection of the Tripolitan army.

It should always be remembered what those brief and seemingly insignificant words imply, that "the blockade could be maintained vigorously." It meant that the officers and men suffered endless hardship, in little wooden ships heaving and rolling on stormy seas, their days filled with hard work and dull discomfort.

Those ships always leaked in bad weather, both below the water line and above, for the seams worked with the motion of the ship, opening and shutting as the ship strained on the waves. Every day there would be dreary hours of work on the pumps. Bedding and clothing would always be a little damp.

At any hour of the day or night the watch on deck, and sometimes all hands, would be called upon to hurry aloft to shorten sail or to make more sail. They would clamber about, a hundred feet above the deck, in lashing rain and often in pitch darkness for an hour or two of exhausting labor.

The damp hammocks to which the men could return to rest were crowded together. In the big spar-decked frigates the men could consider themselves lucky; each could sling his hammock in a space fully thirty inches wide, under a deck nearly six feet high. In the brigs and schooners the crowding was much worse—the men might be restricted to a space less than two feet wide for each hammock, under a deck no more than five feet six inches high. They might actually sling their hammocks in two layers; the least lifting of the head when lying there meant bumping it on the man above, or the deck above, according to which layer one happened to be lying in.

Overhead the hatches would be closed tight to keep out the sea that broke over the deck, and the packed mass of humanity below would swing, all together, with the movement of the ship. The smell of the stores and the bilge water would come up from below, and the rats would scurry about, their squeaks plainly to be heard above the snoring of the men and the groaning of the woodwork.

The seamen faced months of this life at a time, with only salted food to sustain them, and the officers were hardly better off. They were nearly as cramped and crowded, nearly as damp as the crews. Then too, they had the responsibility of keeping the ship off the rocks and shoals of one of the most dangerous coasts in the world. They had to hold her in a position from which she could cut off the blockade runners that sneaked among the shoals during good weather.

A commander needed a resolute mind to subject himself and his men to these hardships, especially when it was easy to think up some excuse to return to the peace and comfort of the harbors of Malta or Syracuse. It was hardly to be wondered at that, at the end of that winter, 1804–05, Commodore Barron found his health giving way, so that he had to turn over the command to Captain John Rodgers—the fifth commander-in-chief in four years.

Rodgers in his turn took on the duty of forcing the stubborn Tripolitans to sue for peace. But during that winter a fresh enterprise had been set in motion which might bring the war to an end. It is interesting to note that until this time, after four years of war, President Jefferson, although he was a brilliant man, had not come to appreciate one of the necessary factors in the employment of sea power.

Command of the sea implies a great deal. The power

that commands the sea can send its ships where it wishes, and it can prevent the weaker power from sending its ships to sea at all—in each case, of course, subject to the few exceptions of raiders and blockade runners. The stronger power can gradually wear down its enemy by compelling the weaker power to use up its resources. Jefferson saw this clearly enough. But nearly always sea power, to make itself fully felt, needs the help of military force. In 1945, when the American Navy had won the command of the sea from the Japanese, the capture of Okinawa by the American 10th Army enormously increased the pressure that would be brought to bear on Japan both by sea and air.

And thanks to sea power, the military force need not be very large. Sea power can transport an army quickly and secretly, to strike at any point. The power which is weaker at sea cannot guard against these blows very effectively. During World War II Japan had many more than a million men available whom she would gladly have employed at Okinawa if the American Navy had allowed her to.

In the same way, an army could have been profitably used against Tripoli. The moment the war began America should have dispatched a small army to North Africa. Only from five to ten thousand men would have been needed to defeat the Tripolitan army in battle. Landing an American army on the rugged African coast near enough to make a prompt attack on the city would have been difficult, but it could have been done.

Siege artillery would have been needed to breach the walls of the city ready for the troops to assault, but that would not have been hard to provide. Probably it would never have had to be employed. If when Dale first arrived off Tripoli, the Tripolitans had heard that he had ten thousand men and a siege train ready to land, the Tripolitans would have surrendered instantly. They would have agreed to any terms whatever, sooner than endure an attack.

But that was only a dream. There was no chance of Congress in 1801 authorizing the raising of an army of even four thousand men or of agreeing to its dispatch overseas. In those days the whole American army was numbered by the hundreds, not by the thousands. Even so, it was looked upon with great suspicion as a weapon that might some day be used by a tyrant.

It would have been impossible to persuade either Jefferson or Congress that sending out an army with Dale would be cheaper in the end. Didn't everyone expect that Dale would force peace on Tripoli by means of his unaided naval force in a single summer? No one in 1801 believed for a moment that in 1805 America would still be hurriedly building ships and sending them out to continue the war that was so lightheartedly entered upon.

It should also be borne in mind that sending an army overseas is not a business to be lightly undertaken. It calls for much planning and much experience. To transport an army capable of dealing with Tripoli would have needed a fleet of at least a hundred transports, which America could only have collected with difficulty at that time. To keep men and horses in health during a long sea voyage was a hard matter, and to make sure they had every necessity for warfare with them needed much experience.

Then, too, there was always the chance that the army, even when landed, might be wiped out by disease, as England had discovered more than once.

Brilliantly successful landings, like those of General Eisenhower in North Africa in 1942 and in Normandy in 1944, have to be worked for as well as hoped for. They cannot be taken for granted. The Federal government, at the time of the blockade of Tripoli, did not have the necessary staff to direct and organize an amphibious expedition on any scale, small or large.

CHAPTER 10

EATON ATTACKS BY LAND ACROSS DESERT

IN SPITE OF THE STRONG FEELING AGAINST an army, the idea of striking at Tripoli by a land force supported by the Navy had long been in existence. William Eaton (he usually called himself "general" but the American government was always careful to speak of him as "Mr.") had been United States consul in North Africa for a considerable time. His appointment dated back to 1797, and he had been there off and on since 1799. During that time he had acquired a good deal of experience of North African politics. He was a busy, active man; the suggestions he pressed upon Dale and Morris were among the distractions those unfortunate men had to contend with.

Eaton had ideas about the employment of a land force. So had James L. Cathcart, who had an even more intimate knowledge of North Africa, because he had been a prisoner in Algiers for ten years. There he had become secretary to the Dey (thanks to his knowledge of languages), and from 1799 had been United States consul in Tripoli. Cathcart and Eaton had done much to stir up enemies against Tripoli. They had played a part in the negotiations which had opened the ports of Naples to the American Navy and which had secured the help of the Neapolitan gunboats. Cathcart and Eaton had also hoped at times to secure the services of a Neapolitan army. They were both aware of the existence of a man who might be employed to bring pressure on the Pasha of Tripoli.

This man was Hamet, who might be described as a prince of the royal house of Tripoli. His father had been the bloodthirsty Ali Karamanli, who had managed to maintain himself as Pasha for thirty years, and even to die a natural death in the end.

After Ali's death in 1796, his youngest son, Yusuf, had seized the throne. Yusuf caught one of his elder brothers and murdered him. Another brother, Hamet, managed to escape to Tunis, where he stayed for some time. This worried Yusuf, who was always afraid that Hamet might be used as a figurehead for a rebellion against him. Yusuf made tempting offers to try to get Hamet into his clutches, but Hamet was too cautious.

In the end Yusuf—when the American fleet was in the Mediterranean—offered his brother Hamet a magnificent bribe, nothing less than the half of his kingdom. He appointed Hamet governor of Derna, the chief town of the eastern part of the state. No one can doubt that the offer was made in the hope that sooner or later Hamet would come within Yusuf's reach.

Having been turned out of Tunis, Hamet accepted the offer for he was at his wits' end regarding how to support himself. Then he carefully sailed direct from Malta to Derna without risking an interview with his terrible brother. The odd situation lasted for nearly a year, and then Hamet, quite certain that Yusuf was still scheming for his murder, attempted to rebel, was defeated, and only just escaped with his life. He went to Egypt, and there once more faced the problem of how to get enough to eat.

Eaton and Cathcart had long had their eye on Hamet. The golden opportunity had passed, which was when he was actually in rebellion at Derna. At that time Eaton was in the United States, pressing his scheme upon the administration. By the time President Jefferson and Secretary of the Navy Smith were convinced of the advantages to be gained by supporting Hamet, he had been appointed governor, had rebelled, and had fled to Egypt. However, this news had not yet reached America. Mr. Madison, as Secretary of State, was at last persuaded it was not "unfair" (that was his own word) to support Hamet against his bloodthirsty and black-mailing brother.

So Eaton returned to the Mediterranean in the spring of 1804, empowered to arrange to act in concert with Hamet. And Rodgers received orders to listen to Eaton's advice on how to use Hamet to the best advantage. It was a little upsetting to find that Hamet had disappeared and had abandoned his government of Derna. Still, Eaton was not going to lose the chance of carrying out a plan he had advocated for the past two years and for which he had already crossed the Atlantic twice. His instructions from the Secretary of the Navy had their effect on Barron (this was before Barron relinquished his command to Rodgers). Isaac Hull, Master and Commandant, with his brig *Argus,* was detailed to help Eaton find Hamet and then to assist in any land campaign that might be waged.

Off went Eaton, aboard the *Argus,* to Alexandria. He found Egypt at the time in a state of complete disorder. The Turks were trying to reconquer the country. The Mamelukes—a gang of military chiefs who had ruled Egypt for centuries before Napoleon's conquest of the country seven years before—were trying to regain their power. Various other officers and officials were trying to establish themselves as independent chieftains. War and disease, famine and poverty, rebellion and treachery, had set the whole country in a turmoil.

The British diplomats present were helpful and reliable. On the other hand, the French diplomats, because France was at war with England, thought it their duty to try to balk every British effort. This was done even though England was trying to subdue Tripoli.

But by the aid of the British diplomats, Eaton succeeded in locating Hamet and eventually in getting into communication with him. He was found to be with the Mameluke army far in the interior.

Persuading Hamet to try to become Pasha of Tripoli was a hard task. The wretched man was afraid that the whole scheme was a plan of his brother's to get him into his power and strangle him. Even if it was not as bad as that, Hamet was still afraid that the Americans might hand him over to Yusuf. His fears for his life made him nervous and difficult to deal with. At one point he even ran away for refuge into the desert. But in the end Eaton persuaded Hamet to meet him in a personal conference, and at that conference persuaded him to join in the attempt.

Eaton was determined that the attempt should be made. He was so set upon it that he made promises in the name of the United States that he had no power to make. The final agreement included the shameful clause that Hamet should repay the United States (when at last he should be ruler of Tripoli) out of the money he would extort from other countries. There was apparently no thought in Eaton's mind of putting an end to the whole disgraceful system of piracy and blackmail.

With the agreement signed, Eaton set about the task of raising an army. This should not have been a very difficult task in Egypt where troops without leaders roamed everywhere, but Eaton had very little money. What he had started out with had already been sadly reduced by the need for bribing Turkish officials.

Eaton afterwards declared that with money he could have raised an army of twenty thousand men, and he was probably right. But as it was, he could only offer promises. He might attract troops of a sort by the promise of a share in the plunder of Tripoli, but to obtain food and weapons and ammunition in that famine-ridden country he needed cash. So it was that Eaton exhausted all his resources in scraping together a few stores.

Yet an army was assembled, if it can be called such. It was made up of Moors and Arabs and Greeks, wild Bedouin chieftains, and some stray Austrian and Italian adventurers. There must have been many moments during the expedition when Eaton felt glad that he had with him a personal bodyguard of seven Marines with Lieutenant Presley O'Bannon and Midshipman Pascal Peck. They were the only trustworthy individuals in the whole force of four hundred men.

The tiny army was gathered in the dreary desert overlooking the sea, not far from a place whose name would not be famous for another hundred and forty years—El Alamein. The *Argus* was sent off to Malta with an appeal from Eaton to Barron for food and weapons and money. Then the mob started on their five-hundred-mile march through the country where so much later Rommel and Montgomery, Germans and British and Italians, were to march and suffer in the African campaigns of World War II.

Eaton's force suffered terribly from hunger and thirst as they struggled along, and it was only natural that discouragement and faint-heartedness should make their appearance. Every man knew that in the event of defeat the best he could hope for was slavery, and at worst he would suffer death by torture.

Hamet himself had never had much enthusiasm for the project. The promises Eaton made lost their appeal to men who were hungry and weary. Eaton faced several mutinies. He had to persuade Hamet against abandoning the expedition and retiring to a quieter life in Egypt.

It is quite amazing that Eaton succeeded in keeping the expedition moving forward even slowly—he must have been a man of most persuasive tongue. There was one occasion when by the slaughter of a camel and sheep he was able to provide what he called a "full ration" for his four hundred men. He must have talked very glibly to have persuaded the four hundred into agreeing with him.

For five weeks Eaton coaxed his army along over the five hundred miles of desert. He even tried to drill them into discipline and order as they marched.

At last they struggled into Bomba, a desolate bay without houses or people. And there, in the nick of time, arrived the *Argus,* to keep the appointment made weeks before. From the *Argus,* and from the *Hornet* next day, Eaton received food and ammunition and, equally important, seven thousand dollars in cash.

It was equally important, but disappointing, that the *Argus* and the *Hornet* could spare Eaton no reinforcement in men. There were no marines available, and the little ships had only enough trained seamen for their own purposes, with none to spare for adventures on land. Eaton would have to make do with what he had.

The whole incident was a striking example of the influence of sea power. Without the promise of ships to meet them, Eaton would never have been able to induce his army to move in the first place. And if by some evil chance Yusuf in Tripoli had been able to regain command of the sea and chase away the American squadron, Eaton and his men would have suffered death in the desert or slavery.

With his army fed and paid, Eaton should have had no difficulty in leading it forward over the remaining sixty miles to Derna. But that did not come to pass. Rumors that the army of Tripoli was on the march for Derna sent the whole force into a panic. The men were terrified of Yusuf's cruelty, and wanted to retreat out of harm's way. By some means, Eaton persuaded them to move forward, and three more days of marching brought the four hundred up to the fortifications of Derna.

The sea front and the eastern side of Derna that faced Eaton's army had been fortified, but not very well. Eaton looked the situation over, and sent in a demand for surrender. This was refused, although people inside the town who wanted to make sure of being on the winning side, no matter who won, sent out messages saying they hoped for Eaton's victory.

There was no time to waste. With the passage of time Eaton's army might melt away and Yusuf's army might arrive. Eaton recognized the fact, and he was a man of energy and resolution.

During this time the *Argus* and *Hornet* were anchored off the town, as had been agreed. Now the little *Nautilus,* with her shallow draft and handy rig, was at hand as well.

Eaton needed artillery to batter the defenses; the squadron had a couple of field guns for him. They were landed on the beach, but above the beach rose a steep cliff. One gun was dragged up by main force, and with a single gun at his disposal Eaton would not delay another minute. He had the gun dragged to a little hilltop and set his Greek gunners to work firing on the fortifications.

At the same time, the *Argus* and the *Hornet* and the *Nautilus* came creeping into the shallows as far as they dared, and opened a steady fire on the waterfront. The enemy blazed away in return, bullets flying and some men dropping.

In the excitement one of Eaton's gunners fired off the gun before the ramrod had been withdrawn after ramming down the shot. The ramrod went sailing off toward the enemy's line. It was quite a sight, no doubt, but it meant that the gun was now useless, and its resounding bang would no longer be heard to encourage Eaton's men and dishearten the enemy. With the gun rendered useless, there was no time to lose. Eaton, who had kept his head clear and his spirits high, called on his men to charge. Forward they went, the handful of marines leading, the Greeks behind them, and the Arabs cautiously following up. Fortunately they were faced by an enemy as undisciplined and as shaky as themselves.

The bold attack turned the scale, as Eaton, much to his credit, had realized was to be expected. The garrison fled, but here and there a man turned back to empty his loaded musket at the attackers. One bullet shattered Eaton's wrist, just too late for it to have any effect on the battle.

Lieutenant O'Bannon and Midshipman George Mann knew the importance of keeping a beaten enemy on the run, and they kept the attack moving. Battery and guns were captured, and the guns were turned on the defenders when they tried to rally in the fortified houses. They fled again, and in a few wild minutes the battle was over. Eaton's army held the town, and the wretched Hamet, still much worried about his future, was installed in the governor's palace.

A price had to be paid for victory. Of the seven gallant marines who had followed O'Bannon and formed the spearhead of the attack, two were dead and one was wounded. In addition, Eaton and several Greeks were wounded.

The crisis was not yet over. Most of the garrison of Derna, having fled from the town, assembled again outside it. And Eaton's boldness and promptness in capturing the town was thoroughly justified by the arrival, scarcely more than a week later, of the Tripolitan army.

Despite his wound, Eaton had to work hard to keep his army fighting. There were numerous skirmishes as the Tripolitans circled about the town and risked timid attacks; but Eaton had the guns of the fortifications at his disposal now. And once or twice the *Argus,* searching along the coast, caught parties of the enemy within range and sent cannon balls into them.

Unlike Eaton, the Tripolitan commander could not inspire his men to risk all in a headlong attack. As a result, Eaton was able to hold on to his conquest, and the

Tripolitan army was faced with the necessity of trying to maintain itself in the desert. No doubt it would have speedily melted away—Eaton thought (and he was probably right) that with a little money he could have induced the whole Tripolitan force to come over to his side—if fresh news had not come from Tripoli at that moment.

CHAPTER 11

PIRATES SUBDUED— PEACE REIGNS ON THE HIGH SEAS AT LAST

PEACE WAS MADE. THE BLOCKADE OF TRIPOLI had been maintained, and prizes had been taken. Reinforcements were still arriving from America, and more were expected. These included gunboats which were American built and American manned and which could be used in a fresh attack on the port. One of these tiny craft was lost with all hands crossing the Atlantic but seven others succeeded in making the passage.

The Tripolitans were growing disheartened, and now they were faced by the appalling threat of an attack by land. They weighed the fact that Eaton had made the fantastic march from Egypt to Derna. What was there to prevent his making the no more fantastic march from Derna to Tripoli? If ships could be collected to transport him by sea he might be at the gates of Tripoli within a week.

Thus ran the Tripolitans' thoughts, for in times of war neither side realizes how serious are the other side's difficulties. So Yusuf was anxious to make peace, and he found to his pleased surprise that the Americans with whom he was dealing were equally anxious. They were not determined on his abdication, or on his death, or on the destruction of the fortifications of Tripoli. It actually seemed as if they would be satisfied with promises. And promises cost nothing.

Within a day or two of the beginning of the new bargaining, Yusuf ceased to look over his shoulder at the fearful menace of his brother's advance on Derna. Yusuf's only problem now was finding out how much the Americans would give him.

Tobias Lear, who had the duty of conducting the

bargaining on the American side, had been George Washington's private secretary. Since 1803, Lear had held the position of Consul General, and was anxious to make a name for himself as a diplomat. It was a temptation to think of himself as the man who made peace when everyone before him had failed. More than once he had pressed upon Preble the acceptance of terms which Preble thought ridiculous. Now he had complete control over the negotiations, for Barron was very ill—more than one letter hints that he was not quite sane.

Lear had the advantage of knowing that he had the support of every man in the American naval force outside Tripoli. They were worried about the three hundred prisoners whom Yusuf had held captive for eighteen months. Any agreement that would set them free had merit in the eyes of their comrades. It was a difficult question.

In war the decision of an officer, often comfortably out of danger, may send other men to their deaths. The public that agrees to war, or that demands war, is demanding at the same time that men should be killed. Many people do not consider that unpleasant fact because they do not know which men shall die.

It is a harder thing to decide that a group of men, whose names are known, shall continue to suffer hardship and captivity, when a word may set them free. That word may cost lives in the future; it may abandon to the enemy what other men have died for, but it is hard not to say it.

The prisoners were not suffering as badly in their confinement as they might have suffered. That is not saying a great deal, for the man who has lost his liberty has lost almost everything already. The enlisted men's hardships were lessened by the generous expenditures of money, by the efforts of the foreign consuls, and by the devoted work of Jonathan Cowdery, the surgeon's mate, and Jacob Jones, the second lieutenant. Six of the three hundred men died. This is a small number when it is remembered that they spent eighteen months in an unsanitary city that had a high death rate.

No officer died; and the officers had some small compensation for the loss of a year and a half out of their young lives. This was brought about by their attendance at what David Porter called the University of the Prison: the classes that Porter started with the aid of textbooks supplied by the Danish consul. Every officer had something to teach, and everyone had much to learn; mathematics and navigation, languages and tactics and seamanship. There were classes in all these subjects and the young men learned much about the theory of their profession.

Daniel Patterson and James Biddle are only two among the many distinguished names of the graduates of Tripoli University, although it can never be doubted that any one of the prisoners would gladly have given all his learning in exchange for liberty. Nor can it be doubted that the chances of peace being made and the chances of being set free were discussed far more frequently than the rules of grammar.

So peace was made. The Tripolitans gave their promises. They promised peace and good behavior. They promised that if by misfortune they should ever again be at war with the United States (despite the other promise), they would agree to an exchange of prisoners and would never again ask for ransom. But this time, just this once, they wanted ransom money, and Lear yielded the point. To liberate the ship's company of the *Philadelphia,* Lear handed over sixty thousand dollars and eighty-nine prisoners.

The Tripolitans were most obliging. They accepted the American promise and actually set free Bainbridge and his men before the arrival of the ransom money. They saluted the Stars and Stripes. The Pasha—the unspeakable Yusuf—gave Lear an audience in his palace.

At the same time the treaty made it inevitable that Hamet and his men, whom Eaton had coaxed from Egypt to Derna, should be abandoned. Eaton succeeded in carrying off by sea Hamet and some of his friends. All the rest of the four hundred, and all the inhabitants of Derna who had been unwise enough to declare for Hamet, were left behind.

There was a promise from Yusuf that he would take no action against these people, but in Derna no one believed Yusuf's promises. At the moment when the rejoicing prisoners were being set free in Tripoli, there was despair in Derna. There was violence, too, and Eaton only succeeded in getting himself and Hamet into the ships under cover of his artillery. When he left the place, the people he left behind were preparing for flight into the desert. They were willing to undergo the awful hardships of the six-hundred-mile track to Egypt rather than trust to Yusuf's promises. Eaton had made them promises as well, and no doubt he had not been empowered by his government to make those promises, but it was a pity.

We do not know what happened in Derna when Yusuf's army marched in, but we hear occasional news of Hamet afterwards. We find Hamet and his fifteen followers living in Syracuse on two hundred dollars a month allowed him by Rodgers. We find Hamet petitioning the President for help, and being awarded twenty-four hundred dollars, which took a year to arrive.

Then came the discovery that Lear had secretly agreed to allow Yusuf to keep Hamet's wife and children for four years as hostages. America exerted herself then to persuade Yusuf to hand them over and provide Hamet with a pension. Next we find Hamet actually reinstated as governor of Derna (no one can ever guess what will happen next when a tyrant rules). Finally Hamet fled away to Egypt again and we hear no more of him.

Yusuf lived on for many years in the verminous splendor of his palace in Tripoli. The man who could out face and outbargain the United States was cunning enough and resolute enough to deal with rebellious soldiers and treacherous admirals.

On the edge of the ebb and flow of the world war that engulfed Europe and eventually involved America, Tripoli lay in a comfortable eddy and no power was able to spare ships or army to keep her in order. Yusuf profited as a neutral, and he profited as an occasional belligerent. Privateers who were not too sure of the legality of their captures sold their prizes to him.

He also speculated with profit in the wartime markets, and he did not cling fervently to his neutrality when confronted by a superior force. In the stress of the War of 1812, the Stars and Stripes disappeared from the Mediterranean save when displayed by an occasional privateer. To reword an old proverb, when honest men fell out rogues made the most of their opportunity.

Then suddenly and dramatically the situation changed. The wars ended, and the enormous fleets which for years had fought each other were now free to punish the Barbary States. The Treaty of Ghent had barely been signed before America decided to deal with the Mediterranean nuisance.

America was elated with the victories won at sea during the war with England. She had a navy that had grown up on the solid foundation laid by Preble, a navy that knew its own worth, commanded by men who had passed the test of war. Mr. Madison and Congress were both ready to fight to maintain the dignity of their country. The ships were ready and the men were ready, and experience had shown the value of time.

A squadron sailed in the spring of 1815. Eleven years after Decatur had crept into Tripoli in the little *Intrepid,* he appeared in the Mediterranean in command of a large force. The list of his ships included the glorious names of the *Macedonian* and the *Guerrière.*

The rapidity of Decatur's movements took the world—especially the pirate world—by surprise. Less than a month after he sailed from New York, the flagship of Algiers was a prize and the Algerine admiral was dead on his own quarterdeck. Five weeks after sailing, Decatur was in Algiers harbor dictating terms of peace.

He then took on fresh water and provisions, and within a month was entering Tunis. Tunis could make no defense, and the world was treated to the extraordinary spectacle of a Barbary State handing over hard cash in payment of reparations for breaches of neutrality. No time was wasted; Tunis yielded and paid up in a week.

In three days more Decatur was off Tripoli, bringing with him the news of what had happened in Tunis and hard on the heels of the news of what had happened in Algiers.

From the quarterdeck of the *Guerrière,* Decatur could look over at the castle and the minarets, at the long reef where he had fought for his life with cutlass against pike, at the harbor where he had won his promotion by burning the *Philadelphia.* And Yusuf could look out from his palace and see the American ships, cleared for action, and meditate on the fact that they were commanded by a man who meant business.

Yet in this, our last sight of Yusuf, we have to accord him some amused respect. He knew he had to yield, but of all the North African rulers he alone succeeded in bargaining with Decatur in the face of all Decatur's guns. Thirty thousand dollars was the sum Decatur demanded in damages; but Yusuf beat him down to twenty-five thousand, and finally clinched the bargain by throwing in a thousand dollars' worth of slaves. We can hardly wonder that Yusuf lived on for many years after that; the man who could get the better of a bargain with Decatur in all the flush of victory was a man capable of dealing with most problems.

But even so, Yusuf tasted humiliation and defeat, with a rapidity that could hardly be believed. Less than six months after Congress had declared war, the bags of gold were being ferried out to the *Guerrière* in Tripoli. The American flag was safe from insult, and American citizens were safe from outrage.

Index

ABOUT THE AUTHOR

C. S. Forester was born in Cairo, Egypt in 1899. He was educated in England and considered becoming a doctor, but soon became more interested in writing novels. Forester was thirty-six when his most famous book, *The African Queen,* appeared. Later this story became a classic film starring Humphrey Bogart and Katharine Hepburn.

Forester's best-known books are sea stories. His depictions of life at sea are vivid and filled with accurate nautical detail. Forester was on a freighter voyage when he created a most remarkable character—Horatio Hornblower, a swashbuckling hero and British naval officer during the period of the Napoleonic Wars. Forester gave his character many small weaknesses (he suffers from seasickness and is shy), and the public loved him and demanded more and more stories. Eventually there were eleven Hornblower novels plus a few short stories. Many of these were later produced for film and television.

In addition to his fiction work, C. S. Forester wrote *Nelson,* a biography, *The Age of Fighting Sail* and *The Naval War of 1812.*

BOOKS IN THIS SERIES

✳ STERLING POINT BOOKS

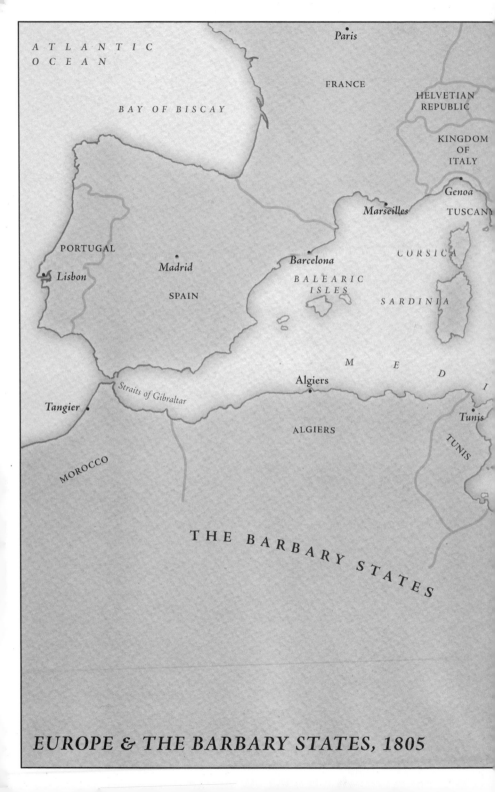

EUROPE & THE BARBARY STATES, 1805